Public Sector Financial Management

Series Editors
Sandra Cohen
Athens University of Economics and Business
Athens, Greece

Eugenio Caperchione
University of Modena and Reggio Emilia
Modena, Italy

Isabel Brusca
University of Zaragoza
Zaragoza, Spain

Francesca Manes-Rossi
University of Naples Federico II
Napoli, Italy

This series brings together cutting edge research in public administration on the new budgeting and accounting methodologies and their impact across the public sector, from central and local government to public health care and education. It considers the need for better quality accounting information for decision-making, planning and control in the public sector; the development of the IPSAS (International Public Sector Accounting Standards) and the EPSAS (European Public Sector Accounting Standards), including their merits and role in accounting harmonisation; accounting information's role in governments' financial sustainability and crisis confrontation; the contribution of sophisticated ICT systems to public sector financial, cost and management accounting deployment; and the relationship between robust accounting information and performance measurement. New trends in public sector reporting and auditing are covered as well. The series fills a significant gap in the market in which works on public sector accounting and financial management are sparse, while research in the area is experiencing unprecedented growth.

More information about this series at
http://www.palgrave.com/gp/series/15782

Isabel Brusca • Patrícia Gomes
Maria José Fernandes • Vicente Montesinos
Editors

Challenges in the Adoption of International Public Sector Accounting Standards

The Experience of the Iberian Peninsula as a Front Runner

palgrave
macmillan

Editors
Isabel Brusca
Department of Accounting and Finance
University of Zaragoza
Zaragoza, Spain

Patrícia Gomes
Department of Accounting and Taxation
Polytechnic Institute of Cávado and Ave
Barcelos, Portugal

Maria José Fernandes
Department of Accounting and Taxation
Polytechnic Institute of Cávado and Ave
Barcelos, Portugal

Vicente Montesinos
Department of Accounting
University of Valencia
Valencia, Spain

Public Sector Financial Management
ISBN 978-3-030-63124-6 ISBN 978-3-030-63125-3 (eBook)
https://doi.org/10.1007/978-3-030-63125-3

This Palgrave Pivot imprint is published by the registered company Springer Nature Switzerland AG.
The registered company address is: Gewerbestrasse 11, 6330 Cham, Switzerland

Preface

During the last years, the International Public Sector Accounting Standards (IPSAS) issued by International Public Sector Accounting Standard Board (IPSASB) have played an important role in the reform and modernization of public sector accounting in many countries. Similarly, the European Union considers that IPSAS can be a reference for the development of European Public Sector Accounting Standards (EPSAS), with the aim of harmonizing accounting systems of Member States. Spain and Portugal have introduced recently the IPSAS into their national accounting standards, which makes interesting to know their experiences.

The aim of this book is to take stock of the experiences of Spain and Portugal in the adoption of the IPSAS, showing the advantages, disadvantages and the main challenges for its implementation. This book can help to understand the level of implementation of the reforms and how governments are applying the IPSAS.

In the first chapter, Tobias Polzer, Christoph Reichard and Giuseppe Grossi analyse the organization of the International Public Sector Accounting Standards Board (IPSASB), with a focus on historic developments, pursued goals and standard-setting processes. Then, they analyse the conceptual framework as issued by the IPSASB.

Tobias Polzer, Giuseppe Grossi and Christoph Reichard, in the second chapter, offer an analysis of the diffusion of the IPSAS in the international framework and the process of harmonization in development in Europe.

Chapter 3, prepared by Patrícia Gomes, Susana Jorge and Maria José Fernandes, analyses the process of adaptation to IPSAS in Portugal. The chapter presents the main advantages and difficulties in the perspective of different actors, such as pilot entities, standard setters, professionals and Court of Auditors. The lack of expertise on the field of public accounting and software's support were appointed as important obstacles.

In Chap. 4, Isabel Brusca, Rosa María Dasí, Amparo Gimeno-Ruiz and Vicente Montesinos, analyse the normative process and the main challenges and benefits that the new system has had in the three levels of government in Spain: central, regional and local. In order to understand the experience of practitioners, a survey for accountants and financial directors has been carried out in the three levels of governments: central, regional and local

In Chap. 5, Isabel Brusca, Patrícia Gomes, Maria José Fernandes and Vicente Montesinos, co-editors of the book, compare the process between Spain and Portugal.

The last chapter presents the main conclusions of the comparative analysis and summarizes the main implications and lessons learned for other countries.

Zaragoza, Spain — Isabel Brusca
Barcelos, Portugal — Patrícia Gomes
Maria José Fernandes
Valencia, Spain — Vicente Montesinos

Acknowledgments

This work was financed by FEDER, Fundo Europeu de Desenvolvimento Regional funds through the COMPETE 2020, Operational Programme for Competitiveness and Internationalisation (POCI), and by Portuguese funds through FCT, Fundação para a Ciência e a Tecnologia, in the framework of the project POCI-01-0143-FEDER-016908 (PTDC/IIM-GES/6923/2014).

Contents

Notes on Contributors

Isabel Brusca is Professor of Accounting in the Department of Accounting and Finance at the University of Zaragoza. Her research and professional interest is focused on public sector accounting and management. She has participated in numerous research projects in this field and is the author of several books and papers in prestigious journals.

Rosa María Dasí is Associate Professor of Accounting and Finance in the Department of Accounting at the University of Valencia (Spain). Her research is mainly focused in the public sector accounting and budgeting and its relations with the National Accounts system. She has participated in several research projects in this field and is the author of several papers in prestigious journals.

Maria José Fernandes is Professor of Accounting in the Department of Accounting and Taxation at the Management School of the Polytechnic Institute of Cávado and Ave. Currently she is the president of the Polytechnic Institute of Cávado and Ave. Her research and professional interest is focused on finance and public sector accounting, particularly on local government accounting.

Amparo Gimeno-Ruiz is Associate Professor of Accounting and Finance in the Department of Accounting at the University of Valencia (Spain). Her research is mainly focused in the public sector accounting, budgeting and management. She has participated in research projects related to financial and management information of local entities.

Patrícia Gomes is Professor of Accounting in the Department of Accounting and Taxation at the Management School of the Polytechnic Institute of Cávado and Ave and a research member of the Research Centre on Accounting and Taxation. She is the coordinator of the post-graduates in the new Public Sector Accounting system based on IPSAS and the researcher responsible for various projects about public sector accounting. She is the author of several papers published in high-quality journals and books in the area of public accounting.

Giuseppe Grossi is Research Professor of Accounting at Nord University, Norway, Kristianstad University, Sweden, and Kozminski University, Poland. His recent publications concern hybrid organizations, smart cities, corruption and migration. He is editor in chief of *Journal of Public Budgeting, Accounting and Financial Management* (Emerald).

Susana Jorge is Associate Professor with Habilitation in the Faculty of Economics, University of Coimbra, Portugal; affiliated researcher of CICP, Centro de Investigação em Ciência Política (Research Centre in Political Science), University of Minho, (Braga) Portugal; researcher in public sector accounting and management, especially focusing on financial reporting and in local government; and chair of the Comparative International Governmental Accounting Research Network.

Vicente Montesinos is Emeritus Professor of Accounting and Finance at the University of Valencia and a registered chartered accountant. He has been dean of his faculty and president of the Spanish Academic Accounting Association. Member of international projects for modernization of public administration, he headed the group of experts for designing a new accounting system of the European Commission. He publishes regularly in indexed scientific journals.

Tobias Polzer is an assistant professor at WU Vienna University of Economics and Business, Austria. His research interests include public (financial) management, public governance reforms and digitalization. His research has been published in *Critical Perspectives on Accounting, Abacus, Public Management Review, International Review of Administrative Sciences* and *Research in the Sociology of Organizations.* He serves as board member of the *Journal of Public Budgeting, Accounting and Financial Management*, the *Journal of Accounting in Emerging Economies*, and the *International Journal of Public Sector Management.*

Christoph Reichard is Emeritus Professor of Public Management at the University of Potsdam, Germany. His recent research covers performance budgeting, accounting change, HR issues, agencification and managerial reforms. He was chair of the European Association of Public Administration Accreditation (EAPAA) and is co-chair of the annual EGPA PhD Symposium.

Abbreviations

CFS	Consolidated Financial Statements
CNCP	Public Sector Accounting Committee—Comité de Normalização Contabilística Público
DGAL	General Directorate for Local Government—Direção Geral das Autarquias Locais
DGO	Budget General Directorate—Direção Geral de Orçamento
EC	European Commission
ECB	European Central Bank
ECE	Entidade Contabilística Estado
EPSAS	European Public Sector Accounting Standards
EU	European Union
GASB	Governmental Accounting Standards Board
GGAP	General Governmental Accounting Plan—Plan General de Contabilidad Pública
IAS	International Accounting Standards
ICAC	Spanish Institute of Accounting and Auditing—Instituto de Contabilidad y Auditoría de Cuentas
IFAC	International Federation of Accountants
IFRS	International Financial Reporting Standard
IGAE	The Government Comptroller's Office—Intervención General de la Administración del Estado, IGAE
IMF	International Monetary Fund
IPSAS	International Public Sector Accounting Standards
IPSASB	International Public Sector Accounting Standards Board
LEO	Budgeting Framework Law—Lei de Enquadramento Orçamental

NCP-PE	Public Accounting Standard for Small Entities—Norma de Contabilidade Pública para Pequenas Entidades
NPM	New Public Management
OCC	Portuguese Board of Chartered Certified Accountants—Ordem dos Contabilistas Certificados
POCP	General Governmental Accounting Plan—Plano Oficial de Contabilidade Pública
S3CP	Centralized system for Accounting and Public Purchases—Sistema Central de Contabilidade e Compras Públicas

List of Tables

CHAPTER 1

Organization of the IPSASB, Conceptual Framework and Claimed Benefits and Criticisms of IPSAS

Tobias Polzer, Christoph Reichard, and Giuseppe Grossi

Abstract This chapter provides an overview of the organization of the International Public Sector Accounting Standards Board (IPSASB), with a focus on historic developments, pursued goals and standard-setting processes. Second, light is shed on the conceptual framework as issued by the IPSASB. Here, contents and the debate around the framework are scrutinized. Finally, the claimed benefits and criticisms of the International

T. Polzer
WU Vienna University of Economics and Business, Vienna, Austria
e-mail: tobias.polzer@wu.ac.at

C. Reichard
University of Potsdam, Potsdam, Germany
e-mail: reichard@uni-potsdam.de

G. Grossi (✉)
Nord University, Bodø, Norway

Kristianstad University, Kristianstad, Sweden
e-mail: giuseppe.grossi@hkr.se

I. Brusca et al. (eds.), *Challenges in the Adoption of International Public Sector Accounting Standards*, Public Sector Financial Management, https://doi.org/10.1007/978-3-030-63125-3_1

Public Sector Accounting Standards themselves are presented, including the debate from academics and practitioners. The text concludes with an outlook on potential future developments.

Keywords International Public Sector Accounting Standards Board • Conceptual framework • Benefits of IPSAS • Criticisms of IPSAS

1.1 Introduction

The aim of this chapter is threefold. First, the text provides a brief overview of the organization of the International Public Sector Accounting Standards Board (IPSASB), with a focus on historic developments, pursued goals and standard-setting processes. Second, it sheds light on the conceptual framework of the International Public Sector Accounting Standards (IPSAS). Finally, it presents the claimed benefits and criticisms of the IPSAS, as the latter have provoked particularly intense debate from academics (Brusca, Caperchione, Cohen, & Manes Rossi, 2018; Hepworth, 2017) and practitioners alike (ACCA, 2017; PwC, 2014). The chapter concludes with an outlook on potential future developments.

1.2 Organization of the IPSAS Board: History, Goals and Processes

The IPSAS Board is responsible for developing the IPSAS and further resources and provides guidance to public sector entities around the world on general purpose financial reporting (IPSASB, 2011). It is one of four independent standard-setting boards that are supported by the International Federation of Accountants (IFAC). The IPSASB consists of 18 volunteer members, which are representatives from government organizations (e.g. ministries of finance or audit institutions), academia and public sector practice (Schmidthuber & Hilgers, 2018). All board members (including the chair and deputy chair) are recommended by the IFAC Nominating Committee and then appointed by the IFAC Board (IPSASB, 2011). Although 15 members of the board are currently designated by the member bodies of the IFAC (there are 157 members and associates in 123 countries worldwide at present), at least three members must be public members (i.e. representing the wider public interest). Board members serve for an initial term of three years, which may be prolonged for another three years (IPSASB, 2018a). The board is supported by a Technical Director (IPSASB, 2011).

Initially established in 1977, the IFAC aims to harmonize accounting regulations worldwide (Müller-Marqués Berger, 2018). In 1986, the IFAC founded the so-called Public Sector Committee (PSC), which is a permanent committee of experts. The PSC was given authority to issue pronouncements on accounting, reporting and auditing issues in the public sector, in order to pursue the IFAC's mission (Aggestam Pontoppidan & Andernack, 2016). In addition, the PSC publishes guidelines and studies concerning public sector accounting (PSA), taking an international perspective. Accounting and auditing standards were also developed and promoted on a voluntary basis; however, this was of secondary importance (ibid.).

Building on this prior work, the PSC's Standards Project was launched in 1996, driven by the central consideration that the previous approach had not led to accounting harmonization (Müller-Marqués Berger, 2018). This project had the firm aim of developing International Standards for Public Sector Accounting (IPSAS) and can be considered a pivotal point in the work of the PSC (Schmidthuber & Hilgers, 2018). Instead of providing recommendations, it aimed to provide standards with a stronger binding effect. The first IPSAS were issued in 1999 (Jensen, 2016). Given the success of the Standards Project, the PSC changed its self-view into an independent committee for the standardization of PSA. With this, the PSC was renamed as the IPSASB in 2004 (Müller-Marqués Berger, 2018).

The IPSASB's strategic goal is '[s]trengthening public financial management and knowledge globally through increasing adoption of accrual-based IPSAS' (IPSASB, 2015, p. 6). This objective is intended to be achieved by:

- 'Developing high-quality public sector financial reporting standards;
- Developing publications for the public sector (e.g. practice guidelines, studies with empirical values of the financial reporting); and
- Raising awareness of IPSAS and the benefits of their adoption' (ibid.).

To meet this strategic goal, the IPSASB has defined a process model with inputs, outputs and a final outcome (IPSASB, 2015). By drawing on inputs such as stakeholder input and the expertise of IPSASB members, IPSASB technical advisors and further staff, 'high-quality financial reporting standards and other publications for the public sector' are to be developed, next to 'presentations and other outreach activities in order to engage with stakeholders' (ibid., p. 9). This is supposed to lead to the final outcome, namely: '[t]hat decision making and accountability of public sector entities are improved and global fiscal stability and sustainability are enhanced by credible and transparent financial reporting' (ibid.), resulting from using accrual-based IPSAS.

The IPSASB follows a structured, public and participative process of standard-setting (the so-called due process; IPSASB, 2011; Schmidthuber & Hilgers, 2018; Schumesch, De Greef, & De Laet, 2015). First, based on monitored international and national developments and received suggestions, the IPSASB identifies potential new projects for standards. Second, these projects are discussed by both the IPSASB and other boards supported by the IFAC. Third, if a project proves to be relevant, an exposure draft for a new standard is formulated by the IPSASB (with the input of a task force and a project advisory panel). Fourth, the exposure draft is released on the IPSASB's website for comments from the general public. The exposure period generally lasts for 120 days, and received comments are published online as well. Fifth, the responses from the public are reflected upon by the IPSASB. If changes are made to an exposure draft by the IPSASB, it is re-exposed for comments (as per the fourth step). Sixth and finally, the new standard is approved and published. A quorum of two-thirds of the IPSASB members is required for approval.

Regarding its Strategy and Work Plan for 2019–2023, the IPSASB held a consultation in 2018 (IPSASB, 2018b). The proposed strategic objective for this period is to strengthen public financial management (PFM) on the global level through an increasing adoption of the (accrual-based) IPSAS. Five themes are key to fulfilling this objective (ibid.):

- Setting standards on public sector-specific issues (e.g. for natural resources, discount rates or differential reporting);
- Maintaining International Financial Reporting Standards (IFRS) convergence (e.g. updating IPSAS 18, Segment Reporting, for IFRS 8, Operating Segments);
- Developing guidance to meet users' broader financial reporting needs (e.g. by recognizing that users in the public sector may not be satisfied with financial statements alone);
- Promoting IPSAS adoption and implementation (through a considered and active outreach); and

- Advocating the benefits of accruals in strengthening PFM by working with other professional groups and sponsoring organizations to help develop the understanding of the PFM benefits of IPSAS adoption.

1.3 IPSASB: Conceptual Framework

The IPSASB published its *Conceptual Framework for General Purpose Financial Reporting by Public Sector Entities*, following approval at its September 2014 meeting.

The conceptual framework 'establishes the concepts that are to be applied in developing IPSAS and Recommended Practice Guidelines (RPGs) applicable to the preparation and presentation of general purpose financial reports (GPFRs) of public sector entities' (IPSASB, 2014, p. 4). It also provides guidance for the preparers of financial reporting by public sector entities that adopt the accrual basis of accounting.

The conceptual framework should assist the standard-setters in developing consistent and relevant standards and should provide broad guidance to prepare auditors on the resolutions of specific issues that are not yet the subject of specific standards (Christiaens & Neyt, 2015).

The conceptual framework includes a preface, eight chapters and an appendix on the Conceptual Framework Due Process application.

The preface highlights the specific characteristics of the public sector that have been considered by the IPSASB in the development of the conceptual framework, such as:

- The primary objectives of public sector entities (i.e. to deliver services to the public);
- The volume and financial significance of no-exchange transactions (i.e. taxes, transfers etc.);
- The importance of the approved budget;
- The nature of public sector programmes and the longevity of the public sector;
- The nature and purposes of assets and liabilities in the public sector;
- The regulatory roles of public sector entities; and
- The relationship with statistical reporting.

Chapter 1 defines the role, authority and applicability of the conceptual framework. Chapter 2 defines the objectives (i.e. accountability and decision-making) of General Purposes Financial Statements (GPFSs) and makes a distinction between primary users (i.e. citizens; resource providers, such as taxpayers, donors, lenders and others; and legislature and members of parliament) and other users. Chapter 2 also describes the characteristics of financial information, principles, benchmarks and the documents included in financial statements. The information provided by GPFSs should include the following: financial position, financial performance and cash flows, budget information and compliance or other service delivery achievements. Chapter 3 presents the qualitative characteristics of information included in GPFRs (i.e. relevance, faithful representation, understandability, timeliness, comparability and verifiability) and the pervasive constraints (i.e. materiality, cost-benefits and achieving an appropriate balance between qualitative characteristics) on such information. Chapter 4 describes the concept of a reporting entity and its characteristics. The last chapters present the elements (Chap. 5), recognition criteria (Chap. 6), measurement bases of assets and liabilities (Chap. 7) and presentation (Chap. 8) of a financial statement.

Several scholars have been very critical towards the IPSASB's conceptual framework because it is mainly based on the International Accounting Standard Board's (IASB) conceptual framework and is considered to be a translation of IFRS in the public sector (Jones, 2007; Laughlin, 2008; Manes Rossi, Cohen, Caperchione, & Brusca, 2016a; Oulasvirta, 2010). The IPSASB's conceptual framework seeks to consider the specific features of public sector entities, but presents several contradictions in its attempt to get closer to the IASB approach. One of the major criticisms is that IPSAS were developed earlier than the conceptual framework, although this should normally happen in the opposite order (Christiaens & Neyt, 2015). Other scholars have highlighted some benefits of the IPSASB's conceptual framework; an example is given below.

> The Conceptual Framework is an essential part of the territorializing process; it is needed to support the coherence of IPSAS and to provide a theoretical frame on which future standards will be built. However, the Conceptual Framework is also an arena for the mediating role of accounting. (Bisogno, Aggestam Pontoppidan, Hodges, & Manes Rossi, 2019, p. 228)

1.4 Claimed Benefits and Criticisms of IPSAS

Since their introduction, there has been lively and controversial debate—particularly in academia—about the appropriateness and usability of IPSAS in PFM and explicitly in public sector financial reporting. In particular, research has shown that PSA standards need 'to respond to the specific features of public sector entities' (Bisogno et al., 2019; see also Manes Rossi et al., 2016a). After more than 20 years of standard development and implementation efforts, a picture of the perceived benefits and criticisms of the IPSAS (both in general and with regard to particular standards) has emerged (Aggestam Pontoppidan & Andernack, 2016; Christiaens, Vanhee, Manes Rossi, Aversano, & Van Cauwenberge, 2015) and is described below.

Nowadays, a major argument in favour of the IPSAS is their worldwide diffusion among numerous governments and multinational organizations (e.g. the United Nations and European Commission; see e.g. Christiaens et al., 2015). The IPSAS can be considered as an international and widely accepted set of accounting standards. Regarding their broad dissemination, IPSAS proponents argue that there is no need to develop a new and different package of PSA standards, as this would be 'reinventing the wheel'. Proponents also emphasize the appropriate mix of private and public sector principles realized in the IPSAS: while the IPSAS are based as much as possible on well-acknowledged private sector standards, they also reflect necessary public sector particularities. Representatives of the big accountancy firms refer to the advantage that with the establishment of IPSAS, already-existing private sector accounting knowledge can also be used for various reporting issues in the public sector. They also point to the issue of consolidated reporting: the IFRS-based IPSAS make the integrated recognition of assets and liabilities easier and more reliable in core government entities and in state-owned enterprises, for example. Finally, IPSAS advocates argue that having an IPSAS-based harmonized governmental accounting system in all EU member states would contribute to more coherent and comparable national accounts as a basis for macroeconomic policies and fiscal steering (e.g. ACCA, 2017; Makaronidis, 2017).

Nevertheless, these arguments in favour of the IPSAS are not at all generally accepted. On the contrary, some of the mentioned arguments have been called into question and debated by a series of critical perspectives and comments. The most obvious controversial issue is the appropriateness of IPSAS for the various purposes and functions of PFM. Although

IPSAS claim to provide information for decision-making as well as for accountability reasons through the means of reporting (IPSASB, 2018a), critics argue that the main focus of the IFRS-based IPSAS is informing capital investors, rather than primarily informing typical public sector user groups such as service recipients or politicians. In a similar vein, some observers doubt that IPSAS can really serve the special needs of PFM, which requires information on the appropriateness of financial resources for the provision of required public goods and services (Lorson, Haustein, & Beske, 2018). Furthermore, the 'directions' of the accounting perspectives in the public and private sectors differ: PFM puts a great deal of emphasis on the *ex-ante* view on resource allocation (and therefore considers the budget to be essential, while IPSAS do not contribute much to the budget), but private sector accounting is strongly concerned with the *ex-post* assessment of business transactions (e.g. for informing investors) and therefore puts much emphasis on the balance sheet.

Critics of the IPSAS therefore point to the considerable weaknesses of the IPSAS conceptual framework, which does not sufficiently respect the particularities of PSA and particularly not those of the existing political, legislative and governance structures and related user needs (Manes Rossi Aversano, & Christiaens, 2014). Critics from Continental Europe emphasize the strong and rather one-sided foundation of the IPSAS on Anglo-Saxon accounting traditions and their significant neglect of divergent accounting cultures (see e.g. Benito, Brusca, & Montesinos, 2007; Grossi & Soverchia, 2011; Oulasvirta, 2014). The preference of the 'true and fair value' principle for the valuation of assets and liabilities in IPSAS is a case in point for this cultural bias: estimating the fair value is not always easy in the public sector (e.g. with regard to public infrastructure or heritage assets). Furthermore, while emphasis on the present value of assets and liabilities (which is the major focus of private sector reporting) may be important for the short-term decision-making of capital-market-based investors, such a perspective may be less relevant for the public sector (Brixner & Erdmann, 2015). Here, it is argued that the protection of creditors—as well as citizens and legislative budgetary sovereignty—is more relevant. This implies a strong focus on the long-term fiscal sustainability of a country and on intergenerational equity, in order to limit, for example, the debt extension of governments, or prevent an increase in the financial burdens of future generations. Such long-term-oriented cautiousness in the recognition and valuation of public assets, liabilities and revenues is mirrored in the 'asymmetric prudence principle', which plays an important role in the accounting systems of Continental Europe and particularly in Germany (Budäus, Hilgers, & Raupach, 2014; Lorson & Haustein, 2019; Weyland & Nowak, 2016). This approach is explicitly risk averse and may lead to undervaluation of assets. Although such positions may be questionable in the private sector, they seem to be appropriate for the public sector, with its more complex and multifaceted reporting requirements, in order to provide relevant financial information for both decision-making and account rendering (Lorson & Haustein, 2019).

The questionable adequacy of the IPSAS for PSA can be illustrated with two examples. First, Grossi and Steccolini (2015) point to consolidated reporting. IPSAS 6 requests the full control (in terms of ownership) of an entity connected to a public sector organization (PSO) as a prerequisite for being considered as the subject of a consolidated report. Ownership is, however, not the only relevant criterion of the dependence of an organization on a PSO; other variants of dependence also may exist (e.g. dependence via government funding). Yet such dependencies are not recognized by the IPSAS (ibid.). Second, critics have pointed out that the IPSASB seems to prefer to adapt the IFRS to the public sector rather than to provide specific solutions (Oulasvirta, 2014). However, public sector non-exchange transactions cannot be retained as a specific case of exchange transactions, which are the only kind of transaction addressed by the IFRS (Bisogno et al., 2019). Given this, PSA standards must embrace 'publicness' (e.g. Steccolini, 2019).

In the debate on the applicability of IPSAS to public sector financial reporting, several other critical arguments play a role (see e.g. Brusca et al., 2018; Christiaens, Reyniers, & Rollé, 2010; Christiaens et al., 2015; Manes Rossi et al., 2016a):

- IPSAS are not always fully 'internally' coherent, which is the result of the long-lasting and still ongoing process of standard development within the IPSASB since 1997. While some IPSAS were designed more than 20 years ago, others have been published only recently and yet others have been replaced in the meantime.
- Due to their evolution over time, some IPSAS lack a concise conceptual foundation in the conceptual framework, which was only published in 2014.
- IPSAS are based on principles, which means that they provide guidance for the governments introducing them, but still allow too much choice in the process of recognition and valuation. Without

limitations on the various options—for example, by more precise legal prescriptions—sufficient harmonization of governmental reporting across Europe would not be possible (Lorson et al., 2018).

- IPSAS primarily deal with financial reporting and do not provide detailed standards for budgeting and budgetary reporting (Calmel, 2014). Although IPSAS 24 (presentation of budget information in financial statements) gives some recommendations on how to inform about budgeted (i.e. planned) and realized financial items, this standard cannot be seen as a sufficient source of information on how to compose a governmental budget and how to establish budgetary reporting. Thus far, the IPSASB has been very cautious in issuing detailed information on budgeting and the respective reporting, in part because many governments are still hesitating to expand accrual accounting to the budgetary part of their accounting system (Van Helden & Reichard, 2018).
- Critical comments have been made on the governance of IPSAS: here, a key point is the character of the IPSASB as part of the IFAC—that is, as an entity without the legitimation of a (supra-)governmental body or formal authority (CNOCP, 2014; Manes Rossi, Cohen, Caperchione, & Brusca, 2016b). Although some governments are represented in the IPSASB, the entire governance of standard evolution and dissemination is completely 'private'.
- Although the IPSAS have already been introduced (or are on their way towards implementation) by several emerging economies (EEs), the readiness of such countries for the IPSAS may be critically questioned (Hepworth, 2017). Even if external actors such as international donors or consultants are in favour of this change, the use of such a sophisticated reporting concept by public managers or senior bureaucrats is still a critical issue (ACCA, 2017). The mere introduction of new reporting principles is insufficient; rather, an appropriate use of the newly available information is a necessary condition for success. Adding to this, it can be argued that the IPSAS, with their emphasis on enhancing transparency and accountability, may run counter to the objectives of powerful groups in EEs that control violence (e.g. warlords). Recent development theory (e.g. the Access Order theory of development formulated by New Institutional Economists; North, Wallis, Webb, & Weingast, 2013) argues that violence in EEs is controlled by limiting public access to political and economic organizations ('limited access order'). Redistributing rents

(e.g. from state monopolies) to the groups in power provides an incentive for their peaceful cooperation within the existing order (Bunse & Fritz, 2012). The introduction of IPSAS might be at odds with such an equilibrium, as rent-skimming behaviour could be more easily revealed with the resulting increased transparency; thus, implementation incentives are low. Given this situation, it has been argued that development policy should centre on how the state can strengthen its control over violence and, subsequently, on how to create a (legal) framework that eventually leads to an 'open access order' (ibid.). Therefore, the institutional context in EEs might be largely unsuitable for the introduction of IPSAS. When pushed by international donors, IPSAS might hit the targets of the donors but remain superficial—or even be detrimental to development. For example, Lassou concluded in a recent study that formal government accounting reforms, including the implementation of IPSAS, have been used in Benin and Ghana as a façade to hide:

> ...[the] patronage and clientelism [that] abound within an informal setting, which make adopted accounting rules and procedures redundant; hence the observed limited role of accounting in improved accountability, governance, and ultimately development (e.g. poverty reduction). (2017, p. 502)

Critical voices also raise concerns that accounting standards, such as the IPSAS, may serve as tools of the (neo-)colonization of EEs by developed countries by imposing Western accounting standards (Broadbent & Laughlin, 2018; Oakes & Oakes, 2016).

- Last but not least, the costs of the whole accounting change process to shift the existing governmental financial reporting system of a country towards IPSAS are considered to be extremely high and many government representatives doubt if the value for money of this change is positive (Lüder, 2014). For example, the costs of changing the German public accounting concept towards the IPSAS have been estimated at about two billion euros (PwC, 2014). Such concerns are primarily raised by countries where either no change at all occurred or an accrual concept was already established some time ago and where the government is thus afraid of a second intensive change project.

When balancing the arguments for and against IPSAS, the time frame of the critical IPSAS debate must be taken into account. The IPSAS are a moving target: their structure, completeness and focus at PSA have changed considerably over time. In part due to the influence of some of its members, the IPSASB is now more aware of public sector particularities and issues of 'publicness' (Steccolini, 2019; Van Helden & Reichard, 2016), in comparison with a decade ago, for example. This change is manifested in the fact that the IPSASB increased the scope of stakeholder consultations.

1.5 Conclusion

As the critical issues presented here illustrate, the IPSAS have quite a few weaknesses from the perspective of PSA. The foremost criticism is that the IPSAS have been derived from private sector IFRS and thus reflect the circumstances of the public sector in only a limited way. Given the already wide dispersion of the IPSAS, however, it would be unrealistic to strive for a new concept of international PSA standards. A more realistic option would be to attempt to influence the development and formulation of future IPSAS and the revision of the existing standards (Kidwell & Lowensohn, 2019). Counter-balancing the traditionally strong influence of private sector-based accountancy firms on IPSAS development is an important challenge for the academic community involved in PSA. For example, this community should intensively use available opportunities to submit comments to newly designed exposure drafts of the IPSASB. In the past few years, a task force of three academic PSA networks (i.e. the Comparative International Governmental Accounting Research Network [CIGAR] and two special interest groups/permanent study groups—in the European Group for Public Administration [EGPA] and the International Research Society for Public Management [IRSPM]) have taken up this challenge and contributed with extensive comments on and suggestions for several newly developed exposure drafts.

For Europe, there is a new window of opportunity to establish a more appropriate concept of PSA standards: namely, the development of specific European PSA standards—the EPSAS. The ongoing process of drafting a conceptual framework and designing standards in the Eurostat working group raises expectations that a suitable set of common accounting standards will be available at the various levels of European governments in the near future (Makaronidis, 2017).

References

ACCA. (2017). *IPSAS implementation: Current status and challenges*. London: The Association of Certified Chartered Accountants.

Aggestam Pontoppidan, C., & Andernack, I. (2016). *Interpretation and application of IPSAS*. Chichester, UK: Wiley.

Benito, B., Brusca, I., & Montesinos, V. (2007). The harmonization of government financial information systems: The role of the IPSASs. *International Review of Administrative Sciences, 73*(2), 293–317.

Bisogno, M., Aggestam Pontoppidan, C., Hodges, R., & Manes Rossi, F. (2019). Setting international public-sector accounting standards: Does 'public' matter? The case of revenue from non-exchange transactions. *Accounting in Europe, 16*(2), 219–235.

Brixner, H., & Erdmann, J. (2015). Herausforderung EPSAS: Chancen und Risiken aus deutscher Perspektive. *Verwaltung & Management, 21*(5), 251–257.

Broadbent, J., & Laughlin, R. (2018). Accounting as colonisation. In R. Roslender (Ed.), *The Routledge companion to critical accounting* (pp. 205–224). Abingdon, UK: Routledge.

Brusca, I., Caperchione, E., Cohen, S., & Manes Rossi, F. (2018). IPSAS, EPSAS and other challenges in European public sector accounting and auditing. In E. Ongaro & S. Van Thiel (Eds.), *The Palgrave handbook of public administration and management in Europe* (pp. 165–185). Basingstoke, UK: Palgrave Macmillan.

Budäus, D., Hilgers, D., & Raupach, B. (2014). Standardisierung des öffentlichen Rechnungswesens: Vom IMK-Beschluss 2003 zu EPSAS 2015. *Verwaltung & Management, 20*(3), 153–156.

Bunse, S., & Fritz, V. (2012). *Making public sector reforms work. Political and economic contexts, incentives, and strategies. Policy research working paper 6174*. Washington, DC: World Bank.

Calmel, M.-P. (2014). Harmonisation of EPSASs (European Public Sector Accounting Standards): Developments and prospects. *Accounting, Economics and Law: A Convivum, 4*(3), 215–236.

Christiaens, J., & Neyt, S. (2015). International public sector accounting standards. In T. Budding, G. Grossi, & T. Tagesson (Eds.), *Public Sector Accounting* (pp. 23–62). London: Routledge.

Christiaens, J., Reyniers, B., & Rollé, C. (2010). Impact of IPSAS on reforming governmental financial information systems: A comparative study. *International Review of Administrative Sciences, 76*(3), 537–554.

Christiaens, J., Vanhee, C., Manes Rossi, F., Aversano, N., & Van Cauwenberge, P. (2015). The effect of IPSAS on reforming governmental financial reporting: An international comparison. *International Review of Administrative Sciences, 81*(1), 158–177.

CNOCP. (2014). *Réponse du Conseil de Normalisation des Comptes Publics à la question n° 12 de la consultation publique Européenne.* Paris: CNOCP.

Grossi, G., & Soverchia, M. (2011). European commission adoption of IPSAS to reform financial reporting. *Abacus, 47*(4), 525–552.

Grossi, G., & Steccolini, I. (2015). Pursuing private or public accountability in the public sector? Applying IPSASs to define the reporting entity in municipal consolidation. *International Journal of Public Administration, 38*(4), 325–334.

Hepworth, N. (2017). Is implementing the IPSASs an appropriate reform? *Public Money & Management, 37*(2), 141–148.

IPSASB. (2011). *IPSASB fact sheet.* New York: International Federation of Accountants.

IPSASB. (2014). *The conceptual framework for general purpose financial reporting by public sector entities.* New York: International Federation of Accountants.

IPSASB. (2015). *The IPSASB's strategy for 2015 forward: Leading through change.* New York: International Federation of Accountants.

IPSASB. (2018a). *Handbook of international public sector accounting pronouncements. Volume I.* New York: International Federation of Accountants.

IPSASB. (2018b). *Proposed strategy and work plan 2019–2023.* New York: International Federation of Accountants.

Jensen, G. (2016). International Public Sector Accounting Standards (IPSAS). In A. Farazmand (Ed.), *Global encyclopedia of public administration, public policy, and governance* (pp. 1–9). Cham, Switzerland: Springer.

Jones, R. (2007). The functions of government accounting in Europe. *Revista de Estudos Politécnicos. Polytechnical Studies Review, 5*(1), 89–110.

Kidwell, L., & Lowensohn, S. (2019). Participation in the process of setting public sector accounting standards: The case of IPSASB. *Accounting in Europe, 16*(2), 177–194.

Lassou, P. J. C. (2017). State of government accounting in Ghana and Benin: A "tentative" account. *Journal of Accounting in Emerging Economies, 7*(4), 486–506.

Laughlin, R. (2008). A conceptual framework for accounting for public benefit entities. *Public Money & Management, 28*(4), 247–254.

Lorson, P., & Haustein, E. (2019). Debate: On the role of prudence in public sector accounting. *Public Money & Management, 39*(6), 389–390.

Lorson, P., Haustein, E., & Beske, F. (2018). Rechnungslegung im privaten und staatlichen Sektor, Teil 1. *KoR – Zeitschrift für internationale und kapitalmarktorientierte Rechnungslegung, 18*(1), 27–37.

Lüder, K. (2014). *European Public Sector Accounting Standards, Diskussionsergebnisse und Thesen aus wissenschaftlicher Sicht, Vortrag beim Hessischen Rechnungshof, Darmstadt, 02.12.2014.* Darmstadt, Germany: Court of Audit Hesse.

Makaronidis, A. (2017). European Public Sector Accounting Standards (EPSAS). *Accounting, Economics and Law: A Convivium, 7*(2), 1–6.

Manes Rossi, F., Aversano, N., & Christiaens, J. (2014). IPSASB's conceptual framework: Coherence with accounting systems in European public administrations. *International Journal of Public Administration, 37*(8), 456–465.

Manes Rossi, F., Cohen, S., Caperchione, E., & Brusca, I. (2016a). Harmonizing public sector accounting in Europe: Thinking out of the box. *Public Money & Management, 36*(3), 189–196.

Manes Rossi, F., Cohen, S., Caperchione, E., & Brusca, I. (2016b). Introduction: The Gordian knot of public sector accounting and the role of the International Public Sector Accounting Standards. *International Review of Administrative Sciences, 82*(4), 718–723.

Müller-Marqués Berger, T. (2018). *IPSAS explained: A summary of International Public Sector Accounting Standards.* Chichester, UK: Wiley and Ernst & Young.

North, D. C., Wallis, J. J., Webb, S. B., & Weingast, B. R. (2013). Ten lessons – In the shadow of violence. In D. C. North, J. J. Wallis, S. B. Webb, & B. R. Weingast (Eds.), *In the shadow of violence: Politics, economics and the problems of development* (pp. 328–350). Cambridge, UK: Cambridge University Press.

Oakes, H., & Oakes, S. (2016). Accounting colonisation and austerity in arts organisations. *Critical Perspectives on Accounting, 38*(1), 34–53.

Oulasvirta, L. (2010). Public-sector accounting and the international standardization process of presenting financial statements. *Halduskultuur—Administrative Culture, 11*(2), 227–238.

Oulasvirta, L. (2014). The reluctance of a developed country to choose international public sector accounting standards of the IFAC. A critical case study. *Critical Perspectives on Accounting, 25*(3), 272–285.

PwC. (2014). *Collection of information related to the potential impact, including costs, of implementing accrual accounting in the public sector and technical analysis of the suitability of individual IPSAS standards.* Brussels, Belgium: PricewaterhouseCoopers.

Schmidthuber, L., & Hilgers, D. (2018). *IPSAS: History – Spread – Use (Lecture 7 of the DiEPSAm Project).* Rostock, Germany: University of Rostock.

Schumesch, P., De Greef, A., & De Laet, J. (2015). *IPSAS in a nutshell. From principles to practice.* Brussels, Belgium: PricewaterhouseCoopers.

Steccolini, I. (2019). Accounting and the Post-New Public Management: Re-considering publicness in accounting research. *Accounting, Auditing & Accountability Journal, 32*(1), 255–279.

Van Helden, J., & Reichard, C. (2016). Commonalities and differences in public and private sector performance management practices: A literature review. In M. J. Epstein, F. Verbeeten, & S. K. Widener (Eds.), *Performance measurement and management control: Contemporary issues* (pp. 309–351). Bingley, UK: Emerald.

Van Helden, J., & Reichard, C. (2018). Cash or accruals for budgeting? Why some governments in Europe changed their budgeting mode and others not. *OECD Journal on Budgeting, 18*(1), 89–113.

Weyland, B., & Nowak, K. (2016). EPSAS Update: EPSAS als Chance für eine Harmonisierung der Rechnungslegung in Deutschland und in Europa. *Der Konzern, 12*(2016), 558–569.

CHAPTER 2

The Harmonization of Public Sector Accounting and Diffusion of IPSAS

Tobias Polzer, Giuseppe Grossi, and Christoph Reichard

Abstract The aims of this chapter are to take stock of the diffusion of common public sector accounting standards and to set the scene for the subsequent chapters in this book. First, the goals and challenges of harmonization attempts in public sector accounting are outlined. Next, light is shed on the current state of diffusion of the International Public Sector Accounting Standards around the globe. Here, the variations in adoption are also discussed. Finally, a discussion on accounting harmonization in

T. Polzer
WU Vienna University of Economics and Business, Vienna, Austria
e-mail: tobias.polzer@wu.ac.at

G. Grossi (✉)
Nord University, Bodø, Norway

Kristianstad University, Kristianstad, Sweden
e-mail: giuseppe.grossi@hkr.se

C. Reichard
University of Potsdam, Potsdam, Germany
e-mail: reichard@uni-potsdam.de

I. Brusca et al. (eds.), *Challenges in the Adoption of International Public Sector Accounting Standards*, Public Sector Financial Management, https://doi.org/10.1007/978-3-030-63125-3_2

the European Union and the project of developing common European Public Sector Accounting Standards is presented. Further avenues for research are presented.

Keywords Harmonization • Variation in adoption • IPSAS • EPSAS

2.1 Introduction

During recent decades, an important trend in public sectors worldwide has been to adopt private-sector accounting tools (e.g. accrual accounting, consolidated financial statements, cost accounting and performance budgeting; see, e.g. Broadbent & Guthrie, 2008). These changes have been inspired by the ideas conveyed under the umbrella term of New Public Management (Hood, 1991). However, after several years of the enthusiastic adoption of these new concepts and instruments, an increasing number of studies have highlighted the fact that such reforms have not always met expectations (Humphrey, Guthrie, Jones, & Olson, 2005).

The aims of this chapter are to take stock of reform developments and to set the scene for the subsequent chapters in this book. First, the goals and challenges of harmonization attempts in public sector accounting are outlined. Next, light is shed on one particular initiative by examining the current state of diffusion of the International Public Sector Accounting Standards (IPSAS) around the globe. Finally, a discussion on accounting harmonization in the European Union and, in particular, the project of developing common European Public Sector Accounting Standards (EPSAS) is presented.

In terms of terminology we follow Nobes and Parker (2008, p. 75) who understand 'harmonization' in a quite generic sense as a 'process of increasing the compatibility of accounting practices by setting bounds to their degree of variation'. 'Standardization' is different from 'harmonization': While both concepts seek to overcome disharmony or dissonance, harmonization can be seen as a process of reducing existent disharmony without an already fixed final point or goal (Mussari, 2014). Standardization, in contrast, intends to achieve a final target (the standard). And 'unification' of accounting practices can be seen as 'an extreme form of standardization, since it requires a fully fledged standardization' (Mussari, 2014, p. 303).

Finally, we equate 'public sector accounting' with 'public financial management' that comprises the areas of financial accounting and reporting, budgeting and budgetary reporting, management accounting and auditing in this chapter.

2.2 The Harmonization of Public Sector Accounting: Aims and Challenges

Several countries have been moving towards greater homogeneity of private and public sector accounting systems (FEE, 2007; Mussari, 2014). Accounting harmonization in the public sector has been claimed to be desirable for several reasons, the main one being an articulated need for comparability and greater accountability of financial information for stakeholders such as citizens, politicians, public managers, accountants and oversight institutions (Aggestam Pontoppidan & Andernack, 2016).

In the last decades, in order to support these accounting reforms and foster harmonization, the IPSAS Board (IPSASB) has published a set of accounting standards for financial reporting, known as the IPSAS (IPSASB, 2013). The IPSASB was established by the International Federation of Accountants (IFAC), which is the representative organization of the world's professional accounting bodies. By the end of 2018, 40 accruals-based standards for public sector reporting entities had been released (based on the International Financial Reporting Standards [IFRS]), along with one standard for cash-based financial reporting. In 2013, the IPSASB established a conceptual framework.

According to Jones (2007), the IPSAS have been strongly driven by the accounting profession. In addition, for decades, international organizations such as the International Monetary Fund (IMF), the World Bank (WB) and the Organization for Economic Co-operation and Development (OECD) have explicitly attempted to influence the accounting systems of governments that are recipients of loans and grants by these organizations (IMF, 2001). The reform programmes advocated by such agencies and involved credit-rating agencies are considered to be distinctively neoliberal (Ellwood & Newberry, 2007). The IPSAS are believed to be necessary due to the need for reliable information for decision-making purposes in the fields of financial management, control and auditing (e.g. IMF, 2001).

2.3 Diffusion of the IPSAS in the International Context

From a comparative perspective, various countries (both developed and emerging economies) and international organizations (e.g. the European Commission [EC], United Nations, etc.) have implemented the IPSAS, or are currently in the process of adoption (i.e. decision or roll-out stages) (Grossi & Soverchia, 2011). However, in many cases, the IPSAS have been adopted only formally, in parts and/or with amendments to certain standards as issued by the IPSASB; in other words, multiple deviations or 'variations on the IPSAS theme' can be observed around the globe (Benito, Brusca, & Montesinos, 2007; Brusca, Caperchione, Cohen, & Manes Rossi, 2018; Christiaens, Vanhee, Manes Rossi, Aversano, & Van Cauwenberge, 2015; Polzer, Gårseth-Nesbakk, & Adhikari, 2019). Other countries and organizations reject the IPSAS (e.g. German SAI, 2017). Given different degrees of implementation and compatibility of national accounting regulations with IPSAS, a more general question arises: to what extent should government reporting be comparable between countries and, if it should be comparable, can harmonization on a voluntary basis fulfil this purpose (Mattei, Jorge, & Grandis, 2018)?

A number of factors have been reported to influence the diffusion of accounting standards (see Nobes & Parker, 2008 for a general overview of causes and examples of international differences of national accounting systems). Furthermore, there are links between how accounting systems in the private, public and not-for-profit sectors are organized in countries. In order to understand these variations, a range of variables play a role.

First, both IPSAS and national legislations are 'dual moving targets'—that is, they are continuously under development. This makes continuous variations between the standards issued by the IPSASB and national adoption rather the norm than the exception, as standards must be translated into national legislation.

Second, divergence is possible because the IPSAS primarily serve as guidelines for governments to establish their own standards and therefore represent a set of 'soft' standards (Oulasvirta & Bailey, 2016). Governments that are confronted with the decision to implement the IPSAS have a range of options:

- Full adoption of IPSAS as issued by the IPSASB
- Selection of certain standards to be implemented

- Adaptation of standards (e.g. simplification)
- Non-adoption

What is more, some governments pursue a policy of 'sector-neutral' accounting standards (i.e. issuing a single set of accounting standards for the public, private and not-for-profit sectors, or treating transactions the same way, independent of sector; Baskerville & Grossi, 2019; Cordery & Simpkins, 2016).

A third aspect to consider is the type of rule-making body that is responsible for standard setting (Crampton, Dorofeyev, Kolb, & Meyer-Hollatz, 2001; Nobes & Parker, 2008). The following variants are possible:

- Codification of accounting legislation into national law
- Delegation of rule-making to a standard-setting body
- Having the competence for standard setting lie within a government ministry or agency, usually the Ministry of Finance (an advisory board might be established)

It can be assumed that when rule-making is done top-down and centrally by a ministry (and for all administrative tiers), variations may be smaller than when a number of stakeholders or parliaments are involved.

Fourth, a close look at the actual implementation of IPSAS is necessary. Research has shown that despite a substantial formal compliance of disclosure items with IPSAS in some cases, the material compliance lags significantly behind (e.g. a comparison of the original and final budget figures could be legally prescribed but actually missing; see Ada & Christiaens, 2018).

Fifth, the prevailing accounting tradition in a country might serve as a predictor of the implementation of and deviations from the IPSAS. For example, the IPSAS with their emphasis on a 'true and fair view' might be at odds with the prevailing context of 'prudence' (or 'accounting conservativism') in continental European countries (Nobes & Parker, 2008), eventually leading to deviations. Accounting traditions are connected to 'administrative traditions' (see, e.g. Painter & Peters, 2010), as public sector reforms often show similar traits in countries with the same tradition.

In the following subsections, we present an overview of the diffusion of the IPSAS and a selection of examples from adopting countries. We structure the overview alongside the 'administrative traditions' (Painter &

Peters, 2010). The analysis centres on examples from the central government level, while state/regional, local tiers and social funds are not considered.

2.3.1 *Anglo-American Countries*

Australia and New Zealand are regarded as international pioneers in accrual accounting implementation, in terms of both early adoption and proximity of national standards to the IPSAS as issued by the IPSASB. The Australian Accounting Standards Board (AASB; an agency with the Treasury as its parent department) issues financial reporting rules for the public and private sectors, with the aim of developing sector-neutral accounting standards. New Zealand adopted IPSAS-based standards from 2012 onwards (Baskerville & Grossi, 2019), which meant giving up the previous sector neutrality of its accounting standards (however, as the initial IPSAS were essentially IFRS, there were initially not many differences). In the UK, IFRS instead of IPSAS have been chosen for public sector reporting. Nevertheless, IPSAS are taken as an orientation when public sector IFRS are developed further. The United States have not implemented the IPSAS and have no intention to do so in the near future (Sellami & Gafsi, 2019).

2.3.2 *Napoleonic Countries*

In France, public sector reporting standards are quite similar to private-sector standards and only deviate where government specifics apply. The French government is quite sceptical towards the applicability and usefulness of the IPSAS. The French standard-setting board argues that the majority of IPSAS are not directly suitable and would need to be amended or abandoned, as they do not cover the particularities of public sector accounting sufficiently (CNOCP, 2014). Italy, while using a modified accrual-basis system at the central government level, has not adopted the IPSAS. Spain and Portugal have both implemented the IPSAS, albeit to different extents (see following chapters).

2.3.3 *Germanic Countries*

While some Public Financial Management reform activities are currently going on at local and state government levels, the German federal level, with its still-prevailing cash accounting system, is quite sceptical towards accrual accounting in general and the IPSAS in particular (German SAI, 2017). A similar situation can be found in the Netherlands: although accrual accounting is practised at the regional and local level as well as in central government agencies, the Dutch central government still prefers cash accounting. IPSAS are not considered to be relevant thus far (Christiaens et al., 2015). In contrast, Austria introduced accrual budgeting and accounting (aligned with the IPSAS, albeit with some deviations) on the federal level in 2013 (Rauskala & Saliterer, 2015). The deviations of the Swiss federal financial reporting standards from IPSAS are modest. Upon examination of the reasons for Swiss compliance with the IPSAS, it can be stated that the long-standing accounting tradition in the Swiss government (already 40 years of accrual accounting at the Cantonal level) has been quite influential (Bergmann, 2012).

2.3.4 *Nordic Countries*

The Swedish national accounting standards are considered to conform to a great extent to the IPSAS, but the complex structure of the Swedish public sector and a range of political, economic and legal factors prevent full adoption (Tagesson & Grossi, 2015). Finland resisted the implementation of the IPSAS. The most important factor for this decision was the well-developed existing public sector accounting system in Finland that resisted pressures to change (Oulasvirta, 2014). Similarly, Norway and Denmark did not adopt the IPSAS, although Denmark used the IPSAS as an inspiration when developing its own standards (Aggestam Pontoppidan, 2015). Even though the Icelandic accounting system was already quite developed, the Icelandic government decided to implement the IPSAS in 2015. After the financial crisis of 2008, which affected Iceland severely, the IMF supported Iceland's recent decision in favour of the IPSAS (IMF, 2014). At present, the extent of deviations is still being discussed.

2.3.5 *Latin American Countries*

According to Nobes and Parker (2008), the best proxy for predicting the accounting system of a postcolonial country is the system of the former colonial power. Indeed, many countries in South America have followed the examples of the Iberian Peninsula and implemented the IPSAS—albeit to different degrees (Pérez & Hernández, 2007). Cavanagh and Fernández

Benito (2016) clustered countries into four groups: (1) Argentina, Bolivia, Paraguay and Uruguay have not initiated any movement towards the IPSAS; (2) Colombia, the Dominican Republic, Ecuador and Honduras are in the preparation of an implementation strategy; (3) El Salvador, Guatemala, Nicaragua and Panama have developed a reform strategy that includes adopting the IPSAS as a final goal, but have not started the implementation process yet; and (4) Brazil, Chile, Mexico and Peru have started the implementation process. Research, however, has found that implementation of the IPSAS in the countries of the last-mentioned group has been rather inadequate. For example, Brusca, Gómez-Villegas and Montesinos (2016) refer to the case of Peru, where errors were made in valuations (due to a lack of government capacity) during implementation, leaving the project incomplete and rendering it rather a rhetorical exercise.

2.3.6 *Asian and African Countries*

China monitors the ongoing activities around the IPSAS, but currently has no intention to implement them (Chan, 2016). The same is true for Japan and Hong Kong (Sellami & Gafsi, 2019). In Vietnam, a new accounting law was passed in 2017 that requests the adoption of accrual accounting (ACCA, 2017). In the long term, implementing the IPSAS is planned in Vietnam. In Indonesia, accrual accounting was introduced in 2015, influenced by New Public Management philosophy (Prabowo, Leung, & Guthrie, 2017).

In some countries, WB reports were the starting point for the implementation of IPSAS, mostly in the cash-basis form (Adhikari & Mellemvik, 2010). For example, Pakistan and Bangladesh have adopted the cash-basis IPSAS. However, there are no disclosures of accruals and contingencies (ACCA, 2017). Issues such as a lack of training of civil servants, interventions by professional accountants and technical ambiguities inherent in the IPSAS impede the implementation.

The implementation of the IPSAS in Africa (where at least 31 governments have introduced cash-basis IPSAS) seems to be largely an exercise in legitimacy (Adhikari, Kuruppu, Wynne, & Ambalangodage, 2015). These scholars have stated that two key requirements of the cash-basis IPSAS (i.e. development of consolidated fiscal statements and disclosure of support received from donors in kind) have led to an abandonment of adoption in many cases. Lassou (2017) found that the IPSAS and other public sector accounting reforms have created a space for patronage and corruption in Africa, rather than leading to improvements in accountability and governance. In a case study on Tanzania, Goddard, Assad, Issa, Malagila and Mkasiwa (2016) reported that while financial statements were stamped as 'fully IPSAS compliant', this was far from reality.

2.3.7 Former Soviet and Central and Eastern European Countries

From 2004 onwards, Russia embarked on a journey towards the IPSAS. However, the literature reports Russian accounting practices that are decoupled from declared accounting norms (Antipova & Bourmistrov, 2013). Similar to other countries, Russia views the IPSAS as a symbol for gaining international legitimacy; nevertheless, contradictions are seen with the public sector accounting tradition. In contrast, there is an orientation towards the IPSAS in Estonia, with only modest deviations of Estonian standards from the IPSAS (Argento, Peda, & Grossi, 2018). Latvia has embarked on implementing the IPSAS, but before full compliance is possible, there is still a need for an assessment of some national standards and the development of a project plan (ACCA, 2017). While Armenia and Azerbaijan have implemented the IPSAS, Georgia has not (Sellami & Gafsi, 2019).

2.4 EPSAS and Accounting Harmonization in the European Union

2.4.1 The Specific Need for Harmonization Among EU Member States

Harmonization of public sector accounting systems is particularly important for the member states (MS) of the EU, given the strong interconnectedness of their economies and governments with regard to expenditures, revenues and debts (Jorge, Caruana, & Caperchione, 2019). Accounting harmonization is an important prerequisite for the compilation of the national accounts (NA) of all MS and, ultimately, for the assessment of the fiscal situation to be performed and for necessary fiscal measures to be taken by the EC (see e.g. Manes Rossi, Cohen, Caperchione, & Brusca, 2016).

The most essential requirement for harmonization is the preparation of NA by the government authorities of the various EU MS. All governments must report their financial data to Eurostat, the Directorate-General of the EC for statistics, using common formats and rules according to the Excessive Deficit Procedure (EDP) and the European System of Accounts (ESA, 2010). The reporting base are the budgetary reports of the MS, which still mostly follow the cash mode. The transformation of the financial figures from the (microeconomic) governmental accounts (GA) via the Governance Finance Statistics (GFS) to the (macroeconomic) NA, which follow the accruals mode, is complex (Jorge, Jesus, & Laureano, 2016). This conversion—performed by the statistical offices in the MS—is based on various estimates, assumptions and data corrections and may result in errors and distortions (Lüder, 2000). Harmonization of the accounting systems across MS can therefore be seen as an important contribution to higher information quality of NA, at least with regard to the consistency and reliability of the primary data input into GFS. Such an effect can, however, only be expected if harmonization efforts also cover budgetary reporting (as the basis of statistical adjustments). Yet the results of statistical conversion depend upon numerous factors, of which the style and practice of GA are only one part (see Dasí González, Montesinos Julve, & Vela Bargues [2018], who analysed the convergence of GA and GFS and found that accrual budget reporting alone does not result in higher convergence).

2.4.2 Genesis of the EPSAS Project

The idea of improving the quality of primary data for GFS by harmonizing public sector accounting emerged as a side effect of the financial crisis of 2008 (Caruana, Dabbicco, Jorge, & Jesus, 2019). At the same time there were doubts about the reliability and consistency of the NA of certain member governments, as well as some suspicion regarding manipulation of accounts. It was a firm interest of the EC to strengthen fiscal steering and control; one activity in connection with implementing the 'Six Pack' (a package of six fiscal and macroeconomic regulations; EC Directive 2011/85) was the EPSAS project. This project was initiated by the European Parliament, which authorized Eurostat to study the current situation and to develop the necessary strategy and concepts for accounting harmonization. From the beginning, Eurostat favoured the IPSAS as a reference base, because the IPSAS were considered to be the only well-known and already widely implemented public sector accounting standards.

In 2012, Eurostat initiated a public consultation on the relevance and applicability of EU-wide common public sector accounting standards (European Commission, 2012, 2013; for some results, see Sect. 2.4.3). After receiving quite positive responses in general, Eurostat started the EPSAS project by establishing an EPSAS Task Force and by initiating various working groups and cells. In a stepwise manner, the various units develop the concepts and prerequisites for the future establishment of EPSAS. The overall strategy of Eurostat is to follow a two-staged process (Makaronidis, 2017): until 2020, European governments are expected to improve the transparency of their public finances and to move forward towards accrual financial reporting. At the same time, the various working groups should develop the conceptual framework of EPSAS and the necessary governance structures. After that, in a second stage (until 2025), national governments are expected to introduce the EPSAS.

The various groups and cells of the EPSAS Task Force have been quite active over the last few years; they have developed a Conceptual Framework of the EPSAS and prepared a variety of 'issue papers' about different accounting aspects (e.g. on recognition and valuation of assets and liabilities and on reporting formats). Other groups are working on future governance or on first-time implementation.[1] At present, the development of the EPSAS is a work in progress and neither their full content nor their future chances of being accepted by all MS—and eventually mandatorily implemented—can be assessed. Proponents of EPSAS, however, have realized during the debates among practitioners and researchers that the original ambition to adopt the IPSAS as a mandatory set of accounting standards for European governments would not be feasible (European Commission, 2013). Although the IPSAS are still used as guidelines, various changes and adjustments must be made in order to ensure that EU-wide standards focus sufficiently on the particularities of the public sector. In addition, it will be important to formulate standards in a stricter and more binding way in order to overcome the various alternative accounting treatments allowed by the IPSAS.

[1] For details, see: https://ec.europa.eu/eurostat/web/epsas/overview

2.4.3 *Positions of Major Stakeholders Towards EPSAS*

Government organizations from only one third of all MS participated in the 2012 Eurostat consultation. In general, the majority of respondents showed a positive stance towards the IPSAS as a basis for the EPSAS (Aggestam Pontoppidan & Brusca, 2016; European Commission, 2012). However, the respondents that are officially responsible for accounting issues (e.g. the Ministries of Finance) were by and large less positive. The Ministries of Finance of France, Germany, the Netherlands and Poland were particularly critical. Major concerns touched on, for example, the (still) ongoing development of the IPSAS, their quite strong private-sector focus, the too-high degree of alternative accounting treatments and the expensive implementation process.

A recent survey among senior bureaucrats in central government ministries of almost all EU MS showed a somewhat more positive picture (Hilgers, Frintrup, & Raffer, 2018): the majority of respondents were convinced that EPSAS would bring increased comparability of accounting data and strengthened accountability and transparency. Three quarters of the respondents assessed the EPSAS positively, such as with regard to the valuation of assets. However, the EPSAS seem to be less attractive for respondents in countries with long experience with accrual accounting, because such countries fear new reform efforts.

2.4.4 *Perspectives of Accounting Harmonization in Europe*

The EPSAS project has shown interesting dynamics over the last few years. Although legally still unsettled, its attractiveness as a common denominator or guideline for public sector financial reporting for the EC—and for most of the stakeholders—is quite high. Its relationship with the IPSAS is still not fully clear; most probably, both concepts will be related to each other, but will not be identical.

Thus far, the EPSAS—like the IPSAS—focus on financial reporting. As mentioned earlier, the GFS regulations of ESA 2010 do not rely on financial reports, but take budgetary reports as the basis for the transformation of primary data. Thus, as long as the GFS concept of translating GA data into NA does not change, a harmonized financial reporting system within the EU MS will not have much impact on macroeconomic national accounting. There would only be an influence on the GFS if the various European governments were to accept expanding the EPSAS to budgeting and budgetary accounting. Such an expansion seems very unlikely at present, however, as previous studies have shown that most governments are convinced that a cash-based budget with subsequent cash-based reporting is most appropriate for them (Van Helden & Reichard, 2018).

For these reasons, improving the prerequisites for the statistical transformation process in the context of GFS and the EDP is only one objective of the ongoing harmonization efforts in European public sector accounting. Other objectives may be more relevant; for example, a greater comparability of financial data due to harmonized accounting standards may improve the financial relations of the MS and the EC and enhance the creditability of governments on capital markets. An improved quality of public sector accounting data due to harmonized standards also carries positive effect for the suppliers of goods and services and for taxpayers.

2.5 Conclusions

The aims of this chapter were to take stock of the reform developments towards accounting harmonization and to set the scene for the following chapters. To sum up, this chapter described the large variations that can be seen in the current state of IPSAS implementation across the globe. Deviations can occur 'ex-ante' or 'ex-post' implementation: while governments deliberately deviate from implementing the IPSAS as issued by the IPSASB, decoupling between decisions and actual practices can be observed (e.g. in some postcolonial countries). An explanation for the latter form of deviation is that in such cases, the IPSAS have largely been implemented for reasons of legitimacy or due to pressures from donors.

Even if the EPSAS will be codified for all public sector organizations within several years, central questions remain: to what extent will accountants in all of the various public sector organizations across Europe be able and willing to apply such standards in practice? What deviations from prescribed standards must be expected? Will countries' accounting traditions or fiscal pressures lead to variations of the standards and thereby undermine the comparability of financial data? The chapters on Spain and Portugal in this volume give an 'Iberian' perspective on these questions.

References

ACCA. (2017). *IPSAS implementation: Current status and challenges*. London: The Association of Certified Chartered Accountants.

Ada, S. S., & Christiaens, J. (2018). The magic shoes of IPSAS: Will they fit Turkey? *Transylvanian Review of Administrative Sciences, 54*(1), 5–21.

Adhikari, P., Kuruppu, C., Wynne, A., & Ambalangodage, D. (2015). Diffusion of the Cash Basis International Public Sector Accounting Standard (IPSAS) in Less Developed Countries (LDCs) – The case of the Nepali central government. In K. Jayasinghe, N. D. Nath, & R. Othman (Eds.), *The public sector accounting, accountability and auditing in emerging economies* (pp. 85–108). Bingley, UK: Emerald.

Adhikari, P., & Mellemvik, F. (2010). The adoption of IPSASs in South Asia: A comparative study of seven countries. *Research in Accounting in Emerging Economies, 10*(1), 169–199.

Aggestam Pontoppidan, C. (2015). Public sector accounting and auditing in Denmark. In I. Brusca, E. Caperchione, S. Cohen, & F. M. Rossi (Eds.), *Public sector accounting and auditing in Europe: The challenge of harmonization* (pp. 42–49). Houndmills, UK: Palgrave.

Aggestam Pontoppidan, C., & Andernack, I. (2016). *Interpretation and application of IPSAS*. Chichester, UK: Wiley.

Aggestam Pontoppidan, C., & Brusca, I. (2016). The first steps towards harmonizing public sector accounting for European Union member states: Strategies and perspectives. *Public Money & Management, 36*(3), 181–188.

Antipova, T., & Bourmistrov, A. (2013). Is Russian public sector accounting in the process of modernization? An analysis of accounting reforms in Russia. *Financial Accountability & Management, 29*(4), 442–478.

Argento, D., Peda, P., & Grossi, G. (2018). The enabling role of institutional entrepreneurs in the accounting change of a transitional economy. *Public Administration & Development, 38*(1), 39–49.

Baskerville, R., & Grossi, G. (2019). Globalization of accounting standards: Observations on neo-institutionalism of IPSAS. *Public Money & Management, 39*(2), 95–103.

Benito, B., Brusca, I., & Montesinos, V. (2007). The harmonization of government financial information systems: The role of the IPSASs. *International Review of Administrative Sciences, 73*(2), 293–317.

Bergmann, A. (2012). The influence of the nature of government accounting and reporting in decision-making: Evidence from Switzerland. *Public Money & Management, 32*(1), 15–20.

Broadbent, J., & Guthrie, J. (2008). Public sector to public services: 20 years of "contextual" accounting research. *Accounting, Auditing & Accountability Journal, 21*(2), 129–169.

Brusca, I., Caperchione, E., Cohen, S., & Manes Rossi, F. (2018). IPSAS, EPSAS and other challenges in European public sector accounting and auditing. In E. Ongaro & S. Van Thiel (Eds.), *The Palgrave handbook of public administration and management in Europe* (pp. 165–185). Basingstoke, UK: Palgrave.

Brusca, I., Gómez-Villegas, M., & Montesinos, V. (2016). Public financial management reforms: The role of IPSAS in Latin-America. *Public Administration and Development, 36*(1), 51–64.

Caruana, J., Dabbicco, G., Jorge, S., & Jesus, M. A. (2019). The development of EPSAS: Contributions from the literature. *Accounting in Europe, 16*(2), 146–176.

Cavanagh, J., & Fernández Benito, A. (2016). Public accounting and fiscal credibility. In C. Pimenta & M. Pessoa (Eds.), *Public financial management in Latin America. The key to efficiency and transparency* (pp. 183–236). Washington, DC: International Monetary Fund.

Chan, J. L. (2016). Government accounting with Chinese characteristics and challenges. *Public Money & Management, 36*(3), 201–208.

Christiaens, J., Vanhee, C., Manes Rossi, F., Aversano, N., & Van Cauwenberge, P. (2015). The effect of IPSAS on reforming governmental financial reporting: An international comparison. *International Review of Administrative Sciences, 81*(1), 158–177.

CNOCP. (2014). *Réponse du Conseil de Normalisation des Comptes Publics à la question n° 12 de la consultation publique Européenne.* Paris: Conseil de Normalisation des Comptes Publics.

Cordery, C. J., & Simpkins, K. (2016). Financial reporting standards for the public sector: New Zealand's 21st-century experience. *Public Money & Management, 36*(3), 209–218.

Crampton, A., Dorofeyev, S., Kolb, S., & Meyer-Hollatz, W. (2001). *European comparison: UK & Germany. The main differences between UK and German accounting practice.* London/Düsseldorf, Germany: Deloitte.

Dasí González, R. M., Montesinos Julve, V., & Vela Bargues, J. M. (2018). Towards convergence of government financial statistics and accounting in Europe at central and local levels. *Revista de Contabilidad, 21*(2), 140–149.

Ellwood, S., & Newberry, S. (2007). Public sector accrual accounting: Institutionalising neo-liberal principles? *Accounting, Auditing & Accountability Journal, 20*(4), 549–573.

ESA. (2010). *European system of accounts.* European Comission. Available at https://ec.europa.eu/eurostat/documents/3859598/5925693/KS-02-13-269-EN.PDF/44cd9d01-bc64-40e5-bd40-d17df0c69334.

European Commission. (2012). *Public consultation – Assessment of the suitability of the International Public Sector Accounting Standards for the member states. Summary of responses.* Luxembourg: European Commission.

European Commission. (2013). *Towards implementing harmonised public sector accounting standards in member states. The suitability of IPSAS for the member states.* Luxembourg: European Commission.

FEE. (2007). *Accrual accounting in the public sector.* Brussels, Belgium: Fédération des Experts Comptables Européens.

German SAI. (2017). *Special report pursuant to Article 99 Federal Budget Code on the intended implementation of harmonised European Public Sector Accounting Standards (EPSAS) in the member states of the European Union.* Bonn, Germany: Bundesrechnungshof.

Goddard, A., Assad, M., Issa, S., Malagila, J., & Mkasiwa, T. A. (2016). The two publics and institutional theory – A study of public sector accounting in Tanzania. *Critical Perspectives on Accounting, 40*(1), 8–25.

Grossi, G., & Soverchia, M. (2011). The European Commission adoption of IPSAS to reform financial reporting. *Abacus, 47*(4), 525–552.

Hilgers, D., Frintrup, M., & Raffer, C. (2018). *Sind die EU-Staaten bereit für EPSAS?* Berlin, Germany: Institut für den öffentlichen Sektor.

Hood, C. (1991). A public management for all seasons? *Public Administration, 69*(1), 3–19.

Humphrey, C., Guthrie, J., Jones, L. R., & Olson, O. (2005). The dynamics of public financial management change in an international context: Progress or progression of questions, contradictions, and challenges? In J. Guthrie, C. Humphrey, L. R. Jones, & O. Olson (Eds.), *International public financial management reform. Progress, contradictions, and challenges* (pp. 1–22). Greenwich, UK: Information Age Publishers.

IMF. (2001). *Manual on fiscal transparency.* Washington, DC: International Monetary Fund.

IMF. (2014). *IPSAS in Iceland – Towards enhanced fiscal transparency.* Washington, DC: International Monetary Fund.

IPSASB. (2013). *Conceptual framework for general purposes financial reporting by public sector entities.* Toronto, Canada: International Federation of Accountants.

Jones, R. (2007). The functions of government accounting in Europe. *Revista de Estudos Politécnicos. Polytechnical Studies Review, 4*(7), 89–110.

Jorge, S., Caruana, J., & Caperchione, E. (2019). The challenging task of developing European Public Sector Accounting Standards. *Accounting in Europe, 16*(2), 143–145.

Jorge, S. M., Jesus, M. A., & Laureano, R. M. S. (2016). Governmental accounting maturity toward IPSASs and the approximation to national accounts in the European Union. *International Journal of Public Administration, 39*(12), 976–988.

Lassou, P. J. C. (2017). State of government accounting in Ghana and Benin: A "tentative" account. *Journal of Accounting in Emerging Economies, 7*(4), 486–506.

Lüder, K. (2000). National accounting, governmental accounting and cross-country comparisons of governmental financial condition. *Financial Accountability & Management, 16*(2), 117–128.

Makaronidis, A. (2017). European Public Sector Accounting Standards (EPSAS). *Accounting, Economics and Law: A Convivium, 7*(2), 1–6.

Manes Rossi, F., Cohen, S., Caperchione, E., & Brusca, I. (2016). Harmonizing public sector accounting in Europe: Thinking out of the box. *Public Money & Management, 36*(3), 189–196.

Mattei, G., Jorge, S., & Grandis, F.G. (2018). *Comparability in IPSASs – A good example for EPSASs?* Working paper.

Mussari, R. (2014). EPSAS and the unification of public sector accounting across Europe. *Accounting, Economics and Law. A Convivum, 4*(3), 299–312.

Nobes, C., & Parker, R. (2008). *Comparative international accounting*. Harlow, UK: Pearson.

Oulasvirta, L. (2014). The reluctance of a developed country to choose International Public Sector Accounting Standards of the IFAC. A critical case study. *Critical Perspectives on Accounting, 25*(3), 272–285.

Oulasvirta, L. O., & Bailey, S. J. (2016). Evolution of EU public sector financial accounting standardisation: Critical events that opened the window for attempted policy change. *Journal of European Integration, 38*(6), 653–669.

Painter, M., & Peters, B. G. (2010). Administrative traditions in comparative perspective: Families, groups and hybrids. In M. Painter & B. G. Peters (Eds.), *Tradition and public administration* (pp. 19–30). Basingstoke, UK: Palgrave.

Pérez, C. C., & Hernández, A. L. (2007). Latin-American public financial reporting: Recent and future development. *Public Administration and Development, 27*(2), 139–157.

Polzer, T., Gårseth-Nesbakk, L., & Adhikari, P. (2019). "Does your walk match your talk?" Analysing IPSASs diffusion in developing and developed countries. *International Journal of Public Sector Management* 33(2/3), 117–139.

Prabowo, J. W., Leung, P., & Guthrie, J. (2017). Reforms in public sector accounting and budgeting in Indonesia (2003–2015): Confusions in implementation. *Journal of Public Budgeting, Accounting & Financial Management, 29*(1), 104–137.

Rauskala, I., & Saliterer, I. (2015). Public sector accounting and auditing in Austria. In I. Brusca, E. Caperchione, S. Cohen, & F. Manes Rossi (Eds.), *Public sector accounting and auditing in Europe. The challenge of harmonization* (pp. 12–26). Basingstoke, UK: Palgrave.

Sellami, Y. M., & Gafsi, Y. (2019). Institutional and economic factors affecting the adoption of International Public Sector Accounting Standards. *International Journal of Public Administration, 42*(2), 119–131.

Tagesson, T., & Grossi, G. (2015). Public sector accounting and auditing in Sweden. In I. Brusca, E. Caperchione, S. Cohen, & F. Manes Rossi (Eds.), *Public sector accounting and auditing in Europe. The challenge of harmonization* (pp. 189–203). Basingstoke, UK: Palgrave.

Van Helden, J., & Reichard, C. (2018). Cash or accruals for budgeting? Why some governments in Europe changed their budgeting mode and others not. *OECD Journal on Budgeting, 18*(1), 89–113.

CHAPTER 3

The Application of IPSAS in Portugal

Patrícia Gomes, Susana Jorge, and Maria José Fernandes

Abstract This chapter aims to discuss Portugal's experience in using an IPSAS-based accounting system—the SNC-AP. Despite more than 20 years of experience using accrual accounting, Portugal is in its beginning stages of SNC-AP implementation. Starting from a description of the normative process and the reforms implemented by the Portuguese government, this chapter presents the main advantages and difficulties of such a system in the perspective of different actors (pilot entities, standard setters, professionals, and the Court of Auditors). The lack of expertise in the field of public sector accounting and software support are identified as important obstacles. A clear strategic definition of SNC-AP implementation and a better orientation by policy and professional bodies (such as the CNCP, UniLEO, OCC, DGO, and DGAL) are considered important success measures.

P. Gomes (✉) • M. J. Fernandes
Department of Accounting and Taxation, Polytechnic Institute of Cávado and Ave, Barcelos, Portugal
e-mail: pgomes@ipca.pt; mjfernandes@ipca.pt

S. Jorge
Faculty of Economics, University of Coimbra, Coimbra, Portugal
e-mail: susjor@fe.uc.pt

I. Brusca et al. (eds.), *Challenges in the Adoption of International Public Sector Accounting Standards*, Public Sector Financial Management, https://doi.org/10.1007/978-3-030-63125-3_3

Keywords IPSAS • Accounting reforms • Portugal • SNC-AP • Implementation

3.1 Description of the Normative Process

3.1.1 The Portuguese Public Sector Accounting Reform

Public sector accounting reforms in Portugal have been characterized by a long process influenced by accounting changes implemented in other countries (mimetic isomorphism) and developments in business accounting (normative isomorphism). Being a Southern European country, Portugal has a traditional bureaucracy featuring by some particular characteristics such as the "rule by law" approach to management, the formal control of inputs and procedures, centralized hierarchical organizational structures and decision-making processes, and fragmented structures (Araújo & Branco, 2009, p. 563). However, in this particular context, successive Portuguese governments have implemented several administrative reforms in the last three decades (Araújo, 2001; Gomes & Mendes, 2013).

With regard to public sector accounting changes, several reforms have been introduced since the beginning of the 1990s as part of a broader set of new public management (NPM) initiatives. These mainly occurred given the need to change existing practices and implement new standards recommended by international boards and generally applied in the business sector.

The Portuguese government's accounting framework uses double entry combining cash-based budgetary accounting with accrual-based financial and cost accounting. This framework has been implemented since 1997 with the approval of the first Public Sector Accounting Chart of Accounts (Gomes, Fernandes, & Carvalho, 2015; Jorge, Carvalho, & Fernandes, 2008). During the 1990s, the most important accounting changes were implemented in public sector accounting in Portugal, both in the central and local governments, which led to the disclosure of the first balance sheets, income statements, and other financial and budgetary statements at the beginning of the second millennium. This reform took a long time, and great effort and resources were spent to change accounting practices. Twenty years since the beginning of the reform, the local government has notably been more successful in its implementation considering the level of compliance of annual accounts with the then-approved

Local Government Chart of Accounts. Hence, the local government was a pioneer in the implementation of consolidated statements that became compulsory in 2008, with business standards and the International Public Sector Accounting Standards (IPSAS) as references (Gomes, Brusca, & Fernandes, 2019).

The conclusions of the EUROSTAT report confirmed that "at present, accrual accounting has only been implemented in a limited number of entities" (EUROSTAT, 2012, p. ii) although the reform was expected to start in the 1990s and to be accomplished by the end of 2013 (Gomes et al., 2015).

Since 2010, because of an economic and financial crisis and a great dependence on funds lent by the so-called *Troika* (International Monetary Fund [IMF], European Central Bank [ECB], and the European Commission [EC]), the Portuguese government has been pressed to reform its financial information systems in accordance with international requirements and *Troika* recommendations (Gomes et al., 2015). IPSAS started being referred to in 2010 (Order 474/2010) because of the lack of guidance in preparing public sector entity—consolidated accounts (Gomes et al., 2019; Jorge, Brusca, & Nogueira, 2019). This was well expressed in the *Troika Memorandum of Understanding*, which highlighted the need for an overall "strengthening [of] the public financial management framework" by "strengthening risk management, accountability, reporting and monitoring" (Jorge et al., 2019, p. 12). To give an internal sign of tackling these issues, the Portuguese government elaborated the Document of Fiscal Strategy 2011–2015, assuming the need to prepare the whole budgetary and financial reporting of the Portuguese public administration with international accounting standards as a reference.

Under this context of change motivated by different institutional pressures (Gomes et al., 2015) and the introduction of International Financial Reporting Standards (IFRS) in the business accounting system, the Portuguese Ministry of Finance revised the governance of the accounting standard setter (Decree-law 134/2012), creating the *Comité de Normalização Contabilística Público* (CNCP), whose competencies include issuing public sector accounting standards and interpretations with IPSAS as reference, as well as contributing to its development, implementation, and improvement (Jorge et al., 2019). This committee is composed of different major actors representing stakeholders in the process of change: governmental offices related to accounting and budgeting (central and local government), professional accounting and auditing boards, higher education institutions, statistics offices, and expert academics on public sector accounting. These actors represent an important actor network with power of influence on the change processes in Portugal (Gomes et al., 2015; Jorge et al., 2019).

Three years after the CNCP was created, two important legal documents were approved by government: the new *Lei de Enquadramento Orçamental* (LEO—Law 151/2015) and the new IPSAS-based Accounting System—*Sistema de Normalização Contabilística para as Administrações Públicas* (SNC-AP—Decree-Law 192/2015).

The LEO is applicable to the public administrative sector, which encompasses all the departments, services, and entities of the central, regional, and local administration, as well as the social security subsectors, which do not possess the nature and form of enterprises, foundations, or public associations. The main LEO objectives are to establish (i) budgetary principles and rules applicable to the public administrative sector and (ii) the regime for the budgetary process and execution, the accounting and budgetary and financial reporting general rules, and the rules governing budgetary and financial inspection, control, and auditing with regard to the central administration and social security subsector perimeter (article 1).

The scope of budgets and accounts is defined in article 3 and includes the central administration budget, which shall contain the budgets of the public departments, services, and entities and the *Entidade Contabilística Estado* (ECE). The ECE encompasses the set of accounting operations for which the State is responsible, including its general revenues, liabilities, and assets. ECE management is performed by the Ministry of Finance.

One of the most important issues of the LEO is the definition of the general principles of the accounting system (article 62):

i) The State shall organize budgetary accounting for all its revenues and expenditures and financial accounting for all its assets, liabilities, revenues, and expenditures, and shall prepare individual and consolidated budgetary and financial statements that provide a true and appropriate view of the budget execution, the financial position, changes in the financial position, performance, and cash flows.
ii) Public sector entities individually must prepare budgetary and financial statements that provide a true and adequate view of budget execution, the financial position, changes in the financial position, performance, and cash flows.

Moreover, the LEO states that the accounting system shall consist of budgetary accounting, financial accounting, and management accounting in accordance with the current accounting system and the SNC-AP (article 63).

3.1.2 *Description of the New IPSAS-Based Accounting System*

The new System of Accounting Standards for Public Administrations (SNC-AP) was passed in September 2015, embracing a conceptual framework, a multidimensional chart of accounts (PCM), and 27 accounting standards (NCP) (25 NCP address financial accounting and reporting, one for budgetary accounting and reporting and one for management accounting). Additionally, a simplified financial accounting regime has been approved for smaller and micro entities (SME). Some other countries' frameworks (e.g., Brazil, Spain, and France) were also considered for the development of the SNC-AP, similarly to what happened in the previous accounting system. Table 3.1 presents the relationship between the Portuguese public sector accounting standards and IPSAS. It should be noted that the conceptual framework of the SNC-AP follows the main framework used by the International Public Sector Accounting Standards Board (IPSASB). This is considered an important innovation in the new accounting system, as it was missing in the previous system. Otherwise, the PCM is a particular characteristic of some continental European countries, such as Portugal and Spain, associated with the use of codes of accounts to identify the elements incorporated in the financial statements; its multidimensionality is connected to the integration of different codes of accounts for different uses (e.g., financial statements and the national accounts) in the same chart of accounts.

The SNC-AP is to be applied to all departments, services, and entities that form part of the public administrative sector (including local government and social security), as well as the reclassified public entities. The latter are entities which, regardless of their nature and form (e.g., business entities), have been included in each sector considering the scope of public administration as in the European System of National and Regional Accounts (ESA, 2010).

According to the LEO (article 65), by March 31 of the year following that to which the accounts refer, the ECE and all public entities shall individually prepare their respective reporting documents and deliver them to the Ministry of Finance, the government body responsible for overseeing

Table 3.1 Relationship between the Portuguese public sector accounting standards (NCP) and IPSAS

N°	*NCP Title*	*Correspondent IPSAS (IFAC, 2018)*
NCP 1	Structure and content of financial statements	IPSAS 1
NCP 2	Accounting policies, changes in accounting estimates and errors	IPSAS 3
NCP 3	Intangible assets	IPSAS 31
NCP 4	Service concession arrangements: grantor	IPSAS 32
NCP 5	Tangible assets	IPSAS 17
NCP 6	Leases	IPSAS 13
NCP 7	Borrowing costs	IPSAS 5
NCP 8	Investment property	IPSAS 16
NCP 9	Impairment	IPSAS 21 and 26
NCP 10	Inventories	IPSAS 12
NCP 11	Agriculture	IPSAS 27
NCP 12	Construction contracts	IPSAS 11
NCP 13	Revenue from exchange transactions	IPSAS 9
NCP 14	Revenue from non-exchange transactions	IPSAS 23
NCP 15	Provisions, contingent liabilities and contingent assets	IPSAS 19
NCP 16	Effects of changes in foreign exchange rates	IPSAS 4
NCP 17	Events after the reporting date	IPSAS 14
NCP 18	Financial instruments	IPSAS 28, 29 and 30
NCP 19	Employee benefits	IPSAS 39
NCP 20	Related party disclosures	IPSAS 20
NCP 21	Separate financial statements	IPSAS 34
NCP 22	Consolidated and financial statements;	IPSAS 35
NCP 23	Investments in associates and in joint ventures	IPSAS 36 and 37
NCP 24	Joint agreements	IPSAS 37
NCP 25	Segment reporting	IPSAS 18
NCP 26	Budgetary accounting and reporting	Does not exist
NCP 27	Management accounting	Does not exist

Source: Adapted from Jorge (2015)

the entity in question, and the Court of Auditors. The range of reporting documents include (i) a management report, (ii) budgetary and financial reporting statements, and (iii) other documents required by law. Otherwise, the SNC-AP defines the range of financial statements (NCP 1) and budgetary statements (NCP 26), presented in Table 3.2. All of them represent the general reporting of the ECE and public entities overall, with the obligation to obtain the reporting of the State as a whole.

Table 3.2 General accounting regime versus accounting regime for SME

Description	*General accounting regime*	*Accounting regime for small entities (annual budget > 1 M and < 5 M)*	*Accounting regime for micro entities (annual budget < 1 M)*
Conceptual framework	YES, based on IPSAS	NO (a short summary is included in the NCP-PE)	NO
Public sector accounting standards	25 financial accounting standards	One financial accounting standard (NCP-PE which summarizes the 25 financial standards applied to the general regime)	Not applicable
	Budgetary accounting standard	Budgetary accounting standard	Budgetary accounting standard
	Management accounting standard	Management accounting standard	Not applicable
Financial statements (according to NCP 1)	Statement of financial position Statement of financial performance (by nature) Statement of changes in net assets/equity Cash flow statement Notes to the financial statements	Statement of financial position Statement of financial performance (by nature) Statement of changes in net assets/equity Cash flow statement Notes to the financial statements (simplified version)	Not applicable
Budgetary statements (according to NCP 26)	Statement of budgetary performance Expenditures budgetary execution statement Revenues budgetary execution statement Statement of the execution of the multiannual investment plan Notes to the budgetary statements	The same	The same
Management accounting reporting (according to NCP 27)	Periodic reports to the managers Management reports Statement of financial performance	Periodic reports to the managers Management reports	Not applicable
Multidimensional Chart of Accounts (PCM)	YES	YES	NO

A reference should finally be done to the simplified regime for SME approved in 2016 (Order 218/2016). According to this, micro entities are entities with a budget lower than one million euros; because of their small size, they are only obligated to have financial accounting and reporting, applying only budgetary accounting rules. Otherwise, small entities have a budget between one and five million euros. In this case, these entities apply only one standard of financial accounting—the *Norma de Contabilidade Pública-Pequenas Entidades* (NCP-PE) which follows the 25 standards for the general regime—as well as the budgetary accounting and the management accounting standard of the general regime; the PCM is common for small entities and those of the general regime. Despite this simplified regime, it is important to note that when a small or micro entity integrates another public entity (controlling entity), by the consolidation process they should prepare the accounting information using standards and criteria applicable to the controlling entity. Table 3.2 presents the description of the general accounting regime compared with that for SME.

Under the ESA 2010, it is necessary to elaborate the accounts of the State as a whole, which should include (i) a consolidated statement of budgetary performance for the central administration and social security subsectors, prepared using budgetary accounting rules (LEO) and demonstrating the calculation of budget balances, and (ii) consolidated financial statements for the central administration and social security subsectors, containing an estimate of the execution for the current year.

The government shall submit the consolidated budgetary and financial statements to the Parliament (Assembly of the Republic) by May 15 of the year following the one they refer to. The General State Account shall comprise the set of accounts regarding entities that fall within the state budget perimeter and shall comprise a report, budgetary and financial statements, and annexes to financial statements (LEO, article 66). It is important to note that the budgetary and financial statements must adopt the accounting system applicable to public administrations (the SNC-AP). Thereafter, the General State Account, which remains a cash-based budgetary report, shall be submitted to the Court of Auditors for opinion and certification that integrates the information to be sent to the Parliament by September 30.

3.2 Local and Central Government Experience

3.2.1 The Pilot Entities

The initial target for starting SNC-AP implementation for the entire public administration, including local government, was January 1, 2017. For the implementation process, some initiatives were defined by the Ministry of Finance, namely, a period of pilot experimenting, the publication of a manual to help users implement the new standards, and the definition of a staff training plan.

During 2016, according to what was established in the decree approving the SNC-AP, it had to be tested for implementation in a group of pilot entities selected by the Ministry of Finance; other entities who wanted to participate in the piloting experiments had to send a request to the Ministry of Finance for approval (Decree-law 192/2015, article 11). A list of the pilot entities under the Ministry of Finance was published by the *Direção Geral do Orçamento* (DGO) in April 2016 and completed by the *Direção Geral das Autarquias Locais* (DGAL) to include municipalities. Meanwhile, the standard setter CNCP should provide close guidance to these entities by answering questions in a web portal and preparing an implementation manual (Decree-law 192/2015, article 12). Initial training was foreseen for professionals with the support of the *Ordem dos Contabilistas Certificados* (OCC). These procedures became effective in mid-2016.

Nevertheless, the Ministry of Finance, ultimately in charge of the public sector accounting reforms, decided to postpone the implementation of the SNC-AP to January 1, 2018 (Decree-law 85/2016), acknowledging that the appropriate technical, legal, and institutional conditions for public sector entities to prepare the first annual accounts according to the SNC-AP were not yet in place. It was explicit in this decree that in 2017 any entity could voluntarily start experimenting with the new system (article 5). A national implementation and dissemination strategy for 2017 was to be defined within three months (article 4) and was finally published as law in April 2017 (Order 128/2017).

However, these instructions were broad, referring to the need for generalized staff training (a global training plan needing to be prepared by the Ministry of Finance, involving professional institutes and higher education institutions—article 3); adaptation of IT systems (there should be supporting mechanisms for entities to adapt their IT systems, such as integrating with the general system of the Ministry of Finance—article 4); continuous support regarding clarifying issues related to accounting standards, including using a web portal run by the standard setter CNCP (article 5); and the establishment of a technical group to monitor the overall SNC-AP implementation (article 1, no. 3, and article 2). There were no further references to pilot entities, either in legislation or in other public reports, the last one being in a report from the Court of Auditors in March 2017, about the overall state of implementation of the SNC-AP, highlighting that, after a one-year experiment, "pilot entities did not actually work as such" (Court of Auditors, 2017, p. 23).

For the local government, meanwhile, there was yet again another postponement to January 1, 2019, and a second one to January 1, 2020. The former was by instruction of the Local Government Secretary of State, of December 28, 2017, reflected in the State Budget Execution Law 2018 (Decree-law 33/2018, article 79). The latter was by the State Budget Execution Law 2019 (Decree-law 84/2019, article 86). Therefore, it can be said that municipalities may have been experimenting with the SNC-AP since the middle of 2016, with some exceptions even already reporting according to this new system, especially in 2018. According to information provided by the Court of Auditors, the municipality of Cascais is one good example of an entity that initiated the process of change despite the postponement of the law.[1] Nevertheless, the truth is that, municipalities begin the SNC-AP application only since January 1, 2020. So, to this date they are preparing the IPSAS-based accounts for the first time.

Pilot entities seem strategically important to consider in cases where the new accounting and reporting system involves significant innovations and complexities, to be implemented by many diverse entities at the same time. Therefore, it is necessary that some entities experiment with it first in order to get feedback, leading to eventual adjustments to the system to be finally implemented overall (McLeod & Harun, 2014; Ridder, Bruns, & Spier, 2005).

In Portugal, the public sector accounting reform process has been top-down, from the central to the local government, and the use of pilot entities—at both levels of government and within several sectors of the public administration—was considered important. This would allow the standard setter (and ultimately, the government) to gain experience in how to deal

[1] Communication of the Court of Auditors during the conference on "The transparency and rigour of public accounts: the contribution of the SNC-AP" in Barcelos, Portugal, on June 21, 2019.

with the reforms and the problems likely to be encountered, such as proceeding with staff training. The following sections summarize the first experiments of public sector entities as pilots dealing with the innovations and legal requirements of SNC-AP, trying to illustrate how they were behaving toward the implementation of the new public sector accounting system.

3.2.2 *Data Collection and Sample*

The data were gathered from a survey using a questionnaire (Ferreira & Sarmento, 2009; Hill & Hill, 2008) sent to the pilot entities directly, aiming at, among others, understanding how pilot entities were acting (actors, procedures, involvement, commitment, criticalities, etc.) in the implementation of the SNC-AP and what could make the implementation process easier.

The questionnaire surveyed specific matters related to the process of implementing the SNC-AP, such as the following (Nogueira, Jorge, & Ribeiro, 2020):

- Difficulties and commitment in starting the implementation of the SNC-AP.
- Departments and the number of people involved in the process of implementing the SNC-AP.
- Changes in the entity due to the implementation of the SNC-AP.
- Degree of implementation of a set of procedures developed with a view to implement the SNC-AP.
- Type of external support the entity had and the degree of satisfaction with this.
- Type of support the entity considered important to improve the conditions and/or overcome the difficulties in implementing the SNC-AP.
- Type of impact the entity anticipated the SNC-AP could have on its management.
- How the implementation of the SNC-AP should be carried out.

The questionnaire was applied online during the first trimester of 2017 to the 53 pilot entities selected to experiment with SNC-AP implementation.[2] These entities were distributed by different subsectors of the public

[2] According to the Court of Auditors (2016), 12 entities volunteered themselves and the remainder were invited.

administration, also assuring they were using different accounting software and diverse accounting references or plans. There were 35 responses, mainly from heads of financial and accounting departments/services. Table 3.3 summarizes the sample.[3]

As shown in Table 3.4, central and local government pilot entities correspond to 91.4% of the sample. The majority of entities in the sample uses the Chart of Accounts for Public Sector (POCP) (28.6%) and the Chart of Accounts for Local Government (POCAL) (31.4%). Some entities using SNC and IFRS (14.3%) were also surveyed, such as government and municipality business enterprises and reclassified public entities.

Table 3.3 Sample

	Accounting plans							*Total*
Subsectors	*POCP*	*POCAL*	*POCE*	*POCMS*	*POCISSSS*	*SNC*	*IFRS*	
Central administration	9	0	6	1	0	3	2	21 60.0%
Local administration	0	11	0	0	0	0	0	11 31.4%
Regional administration	1	0	0	1	0	0	0	2 5.7%
Social security	0	0	0	0	1	0	0	1 2.90%
Total	10 28.6%	11 31.4%	6 17.1%	2 5.7%	1 2.9%	3 8.6%	2 5.7%	35 100.0%

Key: *POCP* (Public Sector Plan of Accounts), *POCAL* (Local Government Plan of Accounts), *POCE* (Plan of Accounts for Education Sector), *POCMS* (Plan of Accounts for Health Sector), *POCISSS* (Plan of Accounts for Social Security entities), *SNC* (Business Accounting System), *IFRS* (International Financial Reporting Standards)

Table 3.4 Representativeness of the sample

	Population	*Sample*	*Percentage*
Central administration	36	21	58.3%
Local administration	14	11	78.6%
Regional administration	2	2	100.0%
Social security	1	1	100.0%
Total	53	35	66.0%

[3] The data and tables used here all come from the study of Nogueira et al. (2020).

This sample represents 66% of the population, allowing for some representativeness (Table 3.4), so the results obtained can be generalized for all pilots with relative confidence.

3.2.3 Implementation of the SNC-AP in Pilot Entities

The remainder of this section summarizes the first experiments of public sector entities as pilots dealing with the SNC-AP's innovations and legal requirements, trying to illustrate how they behaved during the implementation of the new public sector accounting system (Nogueira et al., 2020). Data collection and the sample will be first described.

i. ***Difficulties and commitment in the SNC-AP implementation process***

Difficulties experienced by pilots in implementing a new accounting system are important to be identified to help entities define a set of actions to minimize or overcome them. Table 3.5 presents the major difficulties in the SNC-AP implementation experience, using a five-level Likert scale (1 [very low] to 5 [very high]).

As pointed out in Table 3.5, the major problems are unsuitable software, insufficient human resources with appropriate qualifications regarding the new public sector accounting standards, and difficulties in interpreting and applying the recognition and measurement criteria of the public sector accounting standards.

The greatest difficulty relates to unsuitable software, with an average importance of 3.42. Of the entities, 25.7% considered this to be an extremely high degree of difficulty, and 22.9% rated it quite high. The second highest difficulty concerns the lack of suitable staff qualifications in terms of the new public sector accounting standards (average of 3.30). Insufficient knowledge of the new accounting system was noted, and entities experienced significant difficulties in understanding accounting concepts and principles (average of 2.79), especially in interpreting and applying the recognition and measurement criteria of the new public sector accounting system (each with an average of 2.91).

The relevant organizations, such as the DGO, the DGAL, the CNCP, and the *Unidade para a Implementação da LEO* (UniLEO),[4] were

[4] UniLEO, the unit created to monitor the implementation of the LEO and the SNC-AP, was created only in April 2017, after this survey had been conducted.

Table 3.5 Difficulties in the process of implementing SNC-AP

	Very low	*Quite low*	*Average*	*Quite high*	*Very high*	*No answer*	*Average*
Insufficient human resources with appropriate qualifications regarding the new public sector accounting standards	4 11.4%	6 17.1%	7 20.0%	8 22.9%	8 22.9%	2 5.7%	**3.30**
Financial restrictions	9 25.7%	3 8.6%	11 31.4%	7 20.0%	3 8.6%	2 5.7%	2.76
Unsuitable software	4 11.4%	5 14.3%	5 14.3%	8 22.9%	9 25.7%	4 11.4%	**3.42**
Leaders resistance to change/innovation	14 40.0%	5 14.3%	10 28.6%	2 5.7%		4 11.4%	2.00
Operational staff resistance to change/innovation	12 34.3%	7 20.0%	7 20.0%	4 11.4%	1 2.9%	4 11.4%	2.19
Operational staff difficulty in understanding the new accounting concepts and principles	6 17.1%	5 14.3%	13 37.1%	8 22.9%	1 2.9%	2 5.7%	2.79
Difficulties in interpreting and applying the recognition criteria of the public sector accounting standards	6 17.1%	3 8.6%	13 31.1%	10 28.6%	1 2.9%	2 5.7%	2.91
Difficulties in interpreting and applying the measurement criteria of the public sector accounting standards	6 17.1%	3 8.6%	13 31.1%	10 28.6%	1 2.9%	2 5.7%	2.91

supposed to support and monitor the whole implementation process in the pilot entities to minimize the impact of the aforementioned difficulties. They should also have assessed their efforts to understand whether the difficulties are genuine or relate to a certain lack of commitment or dedication.

Regarding their commitment in the transition from the previous system to the SNC-AP, the entities themselves acknowledged that overall they were not so committed with the reform—almost one-third of the entities recognized their low commitment to the process (Nogueira et al., 2020).

This was something relevant to be considered by the oversight authorities given the possible negative impact on the SNC-AP implementation and on the usefulness of pilot entities in the process. However, these difficulties most felt by entities did not seem to be related to each entity's level of commitment, but they were quite generalized.

ii. ***Pilot entities' actions for SNC-AP implementation***

At the organizational level, pilot entities involved their administrative-financial departments in implementing the SNC-AP. Despite the variation in the number of people involved in the process, 85.8% of the entities (30) referred to a range of 1 to 6 people. As to the frequency, these people met to work on the matter, and a great disparity was found—37.1% of entities met monthly, 11.4% weekly, and 5.7% every fortnight, three months, or six months. Some entities stated they were having meetings whenever justified, and others said that these meetings never occurred.

In relation to the organizational changes already happening in entities, these were highly incipient. The creation of a working group to deal with the SNC-AP implementation was clearly the most significant alteration, mentioned by 60% of entities. Also standing out were discussions with external consultants, carried out by 22.9%. Provision of additional financial and human resources was residual, considering that only 8.6% of entities said they hired new expert staff in the area, and only 14.3% said they already allocated a budget for expenses associated with the implementation of the SNC-AP. Moreover, organizational changes do not seem to depend on the public administration subsector that the pilot entity belongs to (Nogueira et al., 2020).

Table 3.6 displays the degree of implementation of various procedures facilitating the SNC-AP using a five-level Likert scale (1 [little implemented] to 5 [greatly implemented]).

The low-level implementation of most of these procedures seems to reflect the low commitment of some entities at this stage. The most frequently implemented procedure was the promotion of human resources' participation in training actions, seminars, and conferences about the SNC-AP (average of 3.4), revealing that entities aware of the lack of preparation of their staff were already working to overcome the problem.

Table 3.6 Implementation of procedures facilitating SNC-AP

	Little implemented	*Almost implemented*	*Averagely implemented*	*Considerably implemented*	*Greatly implemented*	*No answer*	*Average*
Holding preparatory meetings, periodically, with those most directly involved	8 22.9%	8 22.9%	7 20.0%	7 20.0%	4 11.4%	1 2.9%	2.74
Promoting the participation of human resources in training actions, seminars, conferences on SNC-AP	2 5.7%	6 17.1%	9 25.7%	12 34.3%	6 17.1%		**3.40**
Consulting CNCP whenever a doubt arises that the entity is unable to resolve	8 22.9%	6 17.1%	10 28.6%	7 20.0%	3 8.6%	1 2.9%	2.74
Adaptation of software	10 28.6%	7 20.0%	7 20.0%	10 28.6%	1 2.9%		2.57
Simulation of records of some accounting operations	14 40.0%	3 8.6%	7 20.0%	9 25.7%	1 2.9%	1 2.9%	2.41
Simulations of financial and budgetary statements	16 45.7%	7 20.0%	3 8.6%	8 22.9%		1 2.9%	2.09

iii. ***Support from external entities***

One of the reasons that motivate entities to be pilots was the possibility of benefiting from more personalized technical support from the standard setter and other supervisory entities (Nogueira et al., 2020). Pilot entities were asked about this aspect to understand whether they used that support and their degree of satisfaction with it. As shown in Table 3.7, the external bodies offering the biggest support to pilot entities are the OCC (74.3%), the CNCP (68.6%), software houses (62.9%), and the DGO (42.9%). The remainder had provided sporadic help. Generally, support has been of technical character.

Regarding the degree of satisfaction (1 [very unsatisfied] to 5 [completely satisfied]) with the individualized support from each external body, Table 3.8 shows a low satisfaction on average.

The bodies giving the most relevant support to pilot entities were the ones they expressed most satisfaction with. Subsequently, the only ones presenting a positive degree of satisfaction, albeit low (slightly above the middle of the scale), were the OCC (3.21), the CNCP (3.23), software houses (3.14), and the DGO (2.56). There was some evidence of pilot entities highlighting fundamentally the support of the OCC, the CNCP, and software houses. This is probably related to the technical difficulties they were experiencing.

Table 3.7 Support from external entities

	Yes	*No*	*Financial*	*Technical*
Portuguese Institute of Certified Accountants (OCC)	74.3%	25.7%		✓
Public Sector Accounting Standard Settings Committee (CNCP)	68.6%	31.4%		✓
Entity of Shared Services of Public Administration (ESPAP)	20.0%	80.0%		✓
Software houses	62.9%	37.1%	✓	✓
Ministry responsible	8.6%	91.4%		✓
Local Government General Department (DGAL)	8.6%	91.4%		✓
Budget General Department (DGO)	42.9%	57.1%		✓
Court of Auditors (TC)	0.0%	100.0%		
Portuguese Institute of Certified Auditors (OROC)	2.9%	97.1%		✓
Regional Office of Finance and Public Administration of the Autonomous Region of Madeira	2.9%	97.1%		✓

Table 3.8 Satisfaction in relation to support from external entities

	Completely unsatisfied	*Quite unsatisfied*	*Satisfied*	*Quite satisfied*	*Very satisfied*	*No answer*	*Average*
Portuguese Institute of Certified Accountants (OCC)	3 8.6%	3 8.6%	9 25.7%	11 31.4%	2 5.7%	7 20.0%	3.21
Public Sector Accounting Standard-Setting Committee (CNCP)		4 11.4%	13 37.1%	8 22.9%	1 2.9%	9 25.7%	3.23
Entity of Shared Services of Public Administration (ESPAP)	8 22.9%	2 5.7%	3 8.6%	4 11.4%		18 51.4%	2.18
Software houses	2 5.7%	6 17.1%	7 20.0%	12 34.3%	1 2.9%	7 20.0%	3.14
Ministry responsible	9 25.7%	2 5.7%	4 11.4%		1 2.9%	19 54.3%	1.88
Local Government General Department (DGAL)	5 14.3%	3 8.6%	3 8.6%			24 68.6%	1.82
Budget General Department (DGO)	7 20.0%	3 8.6%	11 31.4%	2 5.7%	2 5.7%	10 28.6%	2.56
Court of Auditors (TC)	7 20.0%	3 8.6%	1 2,9%			24 68.6%	1.45
Portuguese Institute of Certified Auditors (OROC)		1 2.9%			34 97.1%		2.00

In this context, pilot entities seemed to highlight the OCC for its fundamental role in training human resources; the CNCP for clarifying more specific technical doubts related to understanding accounting concepts and principles and to the interpretation and application of recognition and measurement criteria; and software houses for their efforts in adapting software to the new accounting system. Still, it is notable that 68.6% of pilot entities considered external entities overall were helping them implement the SNC-AP (Nogueira et al., 2020).

iv. ***Factors facilitating the process of implementing the SNC-AP***

Besides the relevance of pilot entities in identifying difficulties related to the implementation process, it was considered crucial that they propose corrective measures which could be implemented when the SNC-AP would be generally adopted. This was perhaps the central reason of pilots in this case.

Therefore, entities were surveyed about what could make the implementation of the SNC-AP easier. They considered it fundamental to be offered support in relation to (Nogueira et al., 2020)

- more precise orientation by the DGO, the DGAL, and/or others;
- training actions by external entities, directed to the specificities of each type of entity (e.g., health sector, education, local authorities, and reclassified public entities);
- the possibility of hiring more accounting staff;
- more precise orientation by the CNCP;
- the provision of an open forum where all pilot entities could share their doubts; and
- joint meetings with bodies responsible for the SNC-AP and pilot entities.

It also stands out that various entities referred to the need to develop specific software as well as the relevant certification.

How pilot entities would act would also depend on the type of impact they would expect the SNC-AP to have on their management. In this regard, most pilot entities considered there may be a positive impact in relation to decision-making, the financial management process, the budget and financial report, transparency, financial and budgetary performance, the budget management process, and internal control. On the contrary, the signed SNC-AP may negatively affect administrative expenses and the complexity of administrative processes (Nogueira et al., 2020).

As to the overall implementation process, pilot entities seemed to agree with the one followed for the SNC-AP. Of the respondents, 77.1% considered that creating a transitory period and using pilot entities facilitate the implementation process, disregarding immediate application to all entities. Additionally, entities did not find it important that progressive implementation, by sector of activity or level of government, would necessarily facilitate the process.

3.2.4 *The Use of Consolidated Financial Statements in the Local Government*

In Portugal, the first consolidated financial statements (CFS) for local governments became compulsory in 2008. Local governments elaborated this information using national standards that took business accounting standards and IPSAS as their reference. Considering that the *Plano Oficial de Contabilidade Pública* (POCP), the first accounting normative approved for public sector, did not establish the principles needed to properly consolidate accounts, a new law was passed in 2007 (Law no. 2/2007) for local governments, which required municipalities holding 100% of the capital of business entities that provide municipal services to prepare consolidated accounts. This law defined the scope and methods of consolidation and became effective in 2008. However, with the implementation of the business accounting system based on IFRS in 2010, an inconsistency was raised between business entities' and public sector entities' CFS.

Consequently, the Order 474/2010 was approved for the public sector to harmonize the consolidation process with the private sector (Gomes et al., 2019). This order was the first step in Portugal toward the introduction of IPSAS for consolidated accounts.

After SNC-AP approval, an entity that controls another entity must present consolidated statements based on IPSAS 35 to 37, corresponding to NCP 22 to 24. The control is verified when the controlling entity (1) has the right to obtain benefits deriving from its involvement with the controlled entity and (2) has the ability to affect the nature or amount of those benefits through the exercise of power. An entity controls another entity if it has (1) power over the other entity and (2) exposure, or rights, to benefits arising from the involvement with the other entity. To sum up, in the standards for consolidated statements, (1) the criterion of control is used to define where consolidated financial statements must be presented, (2) the criterion of control is used to define the controlled entities that must be included in the consolidated statements, and (3) the full consolidation method is used for controlled entities and the equity method for associated and joint ventures.

The study of Gomes et al. (2019) presents a dual perspective about the use and main problems with the CFS in public sector entities: standard setters and financial management professionals. It concludes that, in the standard setters' perspective, "the use of CFS is important to control entities' debts and expenditures and to provide information for the preparation of the National Accounts" (Gomes et al., 2019, p. 6). In their opinion, the consolidation process is highly institutionalized, and the main obstacles in the preparation of CFS have been eliminated. However, different levels of the use of consolidated information have been found among municipalities because of differences in the level of institutionalization of the consolidation process. This is a gradual process that should be slowly introduced to change practices and methods.

In the professionals' perspective (preparers of the information in local governments), more attention should be paid to "the quality of information provided by CFS and to the use of this information for accountability and decision-making purposes" (Gomes et al., 2019, p. 6). To make decisions, politicians and managers usually use other tools and control systems. In their opinion, there is a limited use of consolidated information in practice. Other problems with the use of CFS are (Gomes et al., 2019, p. 7): (1) the unclear criteria for defining the dependent entities (controlled by other) which should be included in CFS, (2) divergences between the financial reporting of public entities from different sectors and accounting regimes and the overall reporting of the government (national accounts), and (3) the accounting principles of dependent entities and the main entity (controlling entity) were not always the same, especially when the dependent bodies were business entities.

3.2.5 *The First Year of SNC-AP Implementation*

i) ***The Perspective of the Court of Auditors***

The Court of Auditors is one of the main actors in the SNC-AP implementation (Gomes et al., 2015). Its main goal is to ensure higher levels of compliance and the transparency of public sector accounts. To facilitate and simplify the reporting of information under SNC-AP standards, the court created, through Order 1/2019, an integrated system which allows reporting in one single moment for different entities and stakeholders and easy consultation of documents submitted by public entities to the S3CP.[5] This order is applicable to all public sector entities that report to the Court

[5] The S3CP is a centralized communication system of accounting reporting, managed and controlled by UniLEO.

of Auditors. Thus, the Court of Auditors reformed the electronic platform to promote the dematerialization of the reporting process; this way, the reporting to the court is made obligatorily in a digital format through the reporting electronic platform. With these new accounting and reporting procedures, the Court of Auditors takes the opportunity to harmonize the reporting process not only for public sector entities but also for other ones in the private business sector that report to this court. Simultaneously, it was necessary to develop a new information system by the Ministry of Finance in articulation with the *Unidade para a implementação da Lei de Enquadramento Orçamental* (UniLEO).

The main goal of this centralized and electronic system is the dematerialization and digitalization of the reporting process (in the three accounting subsystems: financial, budgetary, and management accounting). With these innovations, the objective is to increase the quality and reliability of the accounting information and to reduce errors.

As mentioned previously, in 2019, public sector entities (with the exception of local governments) were required to prepare and present to the Court of Auditors the first annual financial reporting in accordance with the SNC-AP (for the 2018 fiscal year). To realize the state of the art in this matter, an interview was carried out with two officials of the Court of Auditors with competencies in public sector accounting reports. In their opinion, the main uses of the new accounting system are the production of information to help (i) making managerial and strategic decisions, (ii) preparing individual and consolidated accounts, (iii) measuring and evaluating performance, and (iv) communicating the financial results. However, in the auditors' opinion, several difficulties are felt by practitioners in this first implementation of the SNC-AP, the most important being the lack of expertise and training of accounting staff. Other difficulties are problems with the information systems, especially in the articulation with the central reporting electronic platform—the *Sistema Central de Contabilidade e Compras Públicas* (S3CP), the lack of political and top management involvement in the process of change, as well as the resistance to change associated with a bureaucratic culture.

Overall, in their opinion, this first reporting process in accordance with the SNC-AP is still in its early phase, but they noted that services integrated in the State (such as government departments and offices with less autonomy) experienced more difficulties. These entities begin the introduction of accounting changes (toward the implementation of the POCP and accrual-based accounting) later than other sectors of the public administration, making it more difficult to advance with SNC-AP implementation (Gomes et al., 2015). Another group identified with many difficulties is those composed of reclassified entities (government business enterprises and nonprofit entities which integrate the consolidation perimeter), which remain in a transition process from the SNC to the SNC-AP .

Otherwise, the auditors considered that more autonomous services and entities are more advanced in this first reporting process, such as higher education institutions, health services, and some public institutes. This scenario is justified by the positive progress made by these entities in the implementation of accounting changes since the 1990s (Gomes et al., 2015), namely, introducing accrual accounting and financial statements closer to the business model, which determines favorable conditions for more recent changes. Financial costs in the implementation of changes can also be associated with the moderated level of implementation of the SNC-AP in the opinion of the auditors of the Court of Auditors (Jorge et al., 2019).

Considering some data collected by the Court of Auditors in 2019,[6] out of 1745 entities, 51% presented their accounts based on the SNC-AP (893 entities), and 64% used the central electronic platform. The 49% of entities considered "nonadopters" have continued to apply the prior accounting system—the POCP or sectorial accounting plans (public entities from the central government) or the business accounting system (in the case of reclassified entities and government business enterprises). The sample of "adopters" is mainly composed of entities of the SNC-AP general accounting regime; only 20% are small or micro entities within the simplified regime. These statistics show that a considerable number of entities remain in a transition phase regarding SNC-AP implementation. The difficulties identified above about the interconnection of local information systems with the centralized electronic platform as well as the lack of expertise are important reasons for this modest progress in SNC-AP implementation (e.g., reclassified entities usually work with the business accounting system and are not well familiarized with budgeting accounting and other particularities of the public sector accounting system).

Despite this moderate transition to the SNC-AP, the auditors noted an interesting result for the first year, highlighting the need to invest, in the short term, in staff training and in adequate information systems articulated with the central platform. Also, the continuous (internal and external)

[6] In accordance with footnote 1.

monitoring and accompanying of the implementation (where the UniLEO operational plan and the involvement of top managers play a crucial role) and the certification of public sector accounts are considered as strategic measures to ensure the success of the reform. These findings are similar with those obtained in pilot entities, which seem to show an important consensus between the different actors of the public accounting "ecosystem."

ii) ***Statistics Produced by UniLEO***

The UniLEO is also an important actor in the process of accounting change in the Portuguese context. Under the umbrella of the Ministry of Finance, its goal is to assure the implementation of the LEO, helping the State and its services to increase the effectiveness of public policies to improve results. In a June 2019 conference titled "The transparency and rigour of the public accounting: the contribution of the SNC-AP," the UniLEO coordinator highlighted the difficulties in the implementation process of the new accounting system. Among some political and economic factors that can undermine the evolution of this reform, the coordinator emphasized the lack of expertise of civil servants not only on accounting changes but also essentially on the processes and procedures as a whole, which will result in an unfavorable situation concerning SNC-AP implementation. In his opinion, civil servants in public sector accounting should have enough awareness and knowledge of the functioning of the State and its particularities to determine the best solution to recognize and measure each transaction. Thus, the first measure to ensure success is clearly defining the necessary training, at different levels of the hierarchy, and considering the result that one needs. This cannot be an ad hoc process but rather interrelated with the whole strategy for SNC-AP implementation.

Looking at the UniLEO website, one can also find some statistics on the first submission of public sector accounts (2018 fiscal year) using the S3CP and the guidelines defined by the SNC-AP. Data reported in January 2019 show that only about 50% of the entities communicated the data through the S3CP (the great majority was from the central government). In terms of reporting by ministry, the most favorable situation is verified in entities from the Ministries of Internal Affairs (100%), Justice (91%), and Sea (90%). However, these are only composed of a total of 46 entities, which represent a small part of the whole sample of bodies that should use S3CP for reporting public sector accounts (1276 entities, including schools). Otherwise, the Ministries of Defense (10%), Economy (17%),

Table 3.9 Top five ministries with more entities reporting via S3CP

Ministry	*N° of entities in the perimeter*	*N° of entities that report by the S3CP*	*%*
Internal affairs	13	13	100
Justice	23	21	91
Sea	10	9	90
State General Burden	23	20	87
Presidency of the Council of Ministers	11	9	82

Source: www.unileo.gov.pt

and Health (33%) experienced more difficulties in the communication of reports. The most complicated situation is for schools (non-higher education): out of 811 schools, none used the S3CP in 2018. This may be justified by the long delay these entities experience in relation to POCP implementation, which complicates the transition to the new accounting system. The Ministry of Education declared a lower rate of reporting due to the delay experienced by schools. Table 3.9 presents the summary of the top five ministries in reporting via S3CP.

3.3 Critical Analysis of the Advantages and Disadvantages of the SNC-AP Implementation

The IPSAS adoption process in Portugal was mainly influenced by the external context as well as by the business accounting system (based on IFRS since 2010). It started during the international economic and financial crisis of 2009, which considerably affected Portugal, leading the country to require financial assistance by the so-called *Troika* in 2011 and to sign a *Memorandum of Understanding* on specific economic policy conditionality. The loaners, especially the IMF, among others, also pressured for better accountability regarding public sector financial management and accounts, including reforming the existing public sector accounting system toward IPSAS adoption. In addition, changes in the business accounting system accelerated public sector reform, considering the difficulties in producing consolidated accounts, including the consolidated account of the State as a whole.

Public sector organizations in Portugal, despite NPM initiatives, are still rooted in a prevailing bureaucratic logic, which determines their reaction to reforms (Araújo, 2002). Large and significant reforms, such as that in the accounting system, though often legally and centrally imposed (centralization tradition), are known by entities as usually not implemented at once but generally postponed in face of the initially established start date. Therefore, legal approval for a reform does not necessarily imply immediate action or reaction by organizations (Nogueira et al., 2020).

Under this centralized and bureaucratic context, standard setters (CNCP) only "have administrative independence; the Ministry of Finance is ultimately the entity responsible for the issuance of public sector (as well as business) accounting standards in the form of law" (Jorge et al., 2019, p. 2). Therefore, the standard setters prepare the proposal of standards, but these standards should be approved by a decree-law passed by the Ministry of Finance and the government. Within the Continental European accounting tradition, and contrary to what happens in Anglo-Saxon common-law countries, accounting standards in Portugal assume a legal form, making changing them more difficult, as this implies a bureaucratic process of amending the law (Gomes et al., 2015; Jorge et al., 2019). This is typical in Iberian countries where the professional influence is much lower and standard setters work for governments which sanction their actions (Brusca & Condor, 2002).

Thus, many entities might not act proactively but instead expect to be instructed on how to proceed, sometimes via other detailed regulations. When given broad instructions, entities sometimes nominate working groups to study the subject, but the commitment to the change is not genuine, especially when it is imposed and not exactly explained in terms of its usefulness for the entity's management; they tend to claim lack of time, resources, and especially adequate expertise (Nogueira et al., 2020).

As presented in this chapter, pilot entities were considered, namely by the standard setter CNCP, which is important in the process of implementing the SNC-AP. The complexity of the new standards justified the use of an experimental group of entities which could lead external supervising and supporting bodies in identifying main difficulties, overall supporting the SNC-AP implementation process and helping define a global strategy to overcome them. Some advantages and criticisms have been pointed out by those entities:

- Pilot entities considered themselves moderately committed to the transition from the previous system to the SNC-AP, acknowledging they were not yet completely engaged in the process.

- They were experiencing difficulties in implementing the SNC-AP, the main one being insufficient human resources with appropriate qualifications in terms of the new public sector accounting standards, and unsuitable software.
- The difficulties felt by pilot entities were generalized and were not dependent on their degree of commitment.
- They allocated the task of implementing the SNC-AP to their administrative-financial departments, with very few people involved, establishing working groups for this special purpose; however, no significant changes were found in the organizations at the moment of the survey—overall, the degree of implementation of the various procedures related to the SNC-AP was still relatively low; organizational changes in the entities were very incipient, but the creation of a working group to deal with issues related to SNC-AP implementation was highlighted, as well as promoting staff training.
- The external bodies giving the most support to pilot entities were the OCC, the CNCP, software houses, and the DGO; the degree of satisfaction with this support was generally low despite most pilot entities considering that such support has generally helped them in dealing with the SNC-AP.
- Pilot entities considered the process followed for SNC-AP implementation appropriate, thereby considering that creating a transition period and using pilot entities facilitate the process of transition and implementation; however, it could have been better if more precise orientations were provided by the CNCP, the DGO, the DGAL, and other entities; training actions by external bodies were created (OCC, higher education institutions, etc.); they were able to recruit more staff for accounting (public sector certified accountants); and accounting information systems were improved.

The above allowed the presumption that pilot entities' reduced action toward implementing the SNC-AP may have frustrated the expectations of the standard setter leading the whole process. In fact, few pilot entities considered themselves as significantly contributing to the successful general implementation process of the SNC-AP. The least mentioned reason to become a pilot was precisely for the possibility of contributing, with experience gained, to implement the system in other entities. Only 5.7% of the entities considered their own contribution as vital to a successful general implementation of the SNC-AP (Nogueira et al., 2020).

Nevertheless, on the one hand, the implementation of the SNC-AP using pilot entities was unanimously seen as important (both by the standard setter and the entities themselves), and on the other hand, the aforementioned support pilot entities were considered crucial. It stands out that external supporting entities, as mentioned above, should have defined clear strategies to better facilitate the process. However, pilot entities recognized that they were not offered enough means and support; they were in the process mostly by themselves. As also acknowledged by the Court of Auditors (2016), there was a "deficit of coordination and accompaniment" in the implementation process. One sign of this is probably reflected in delays in implementing the SNC-AP, which continues without being accompanied by due support, apart from some guidelines by the Court of Auditors (Instruction 1/2019).

It would have been crucial for pilot entities to better deal with changes and offer relevant feedback to the CNCP and other supervising bodies, as well as express a more committed attitude toward the reforms; it is surely fundamental to give as much support as possible to all entities from now on for a successful SNC-AP implementation.

Considering the opinion of other main actors in the reform, such as auditors, standard setters, and preparers/professionals, several advantages and disadvantages to the SNC-AP can be identified. The main advantages include the improvement of accountability and transparency of public accounts and of the quality of financial reporting, including the elaboration of consolidated statements. The use of information for accountability purposes as well as for decision-making is also identified as an important advantage to the new accounting and reporting system.

The results of a survey conducted on local governments in Portugal (Gomes, Brusca, Fernandes, & Montesinos, 2018) show that the important advantages to the SNC-AP, according to financial management professionals, are improvements in the quality of information, standardization in the disclosure of information, and increased comparability of information. However, they also recognized that several difficulties undermine this process of change. The main obstacle is the excessive bureaucracy in public administrations. In addition, the lack of human expertise in this field, political involvement, and technical support (mainly information systems) are also considered important obstacles to adopting the new accounting model. These findings are in accordance with the pilot entities' feedback. Regarding measures that can be implemented to ensure the success of the reform, professionals highlighted the need to invest in adequate training and human resources to equip entities with appropriate information systems and increase the engagement of managers and politicians. Presented in the following chapter, these results are similar with those obtained in the Spanish context.

These perceptions about the advantages to the new accounting system are also coherent with those expressed by standard setters and professionals in the use of consolidated information (Gomes et al., 2019). Major drawbacks are associated with the reduced use of this information for managerial purposes and decision-making. In their opinion, to make decisions, politicians and managers normally use other kinds of financial and nonfinancial information, which reduce the relevance and usefulness of consolidated financial statements. This scenario can be explained by the use of business standards as a reference to prepare CFS (since 2008) that do not cover some key accounting topics for the government (EUROSTAT, 2012).

Another critical issue concerns the creation and implementation of the ECE as established by the LEO and the SNC-AP. This reporting entity would be responsible for covering the set of accounting operations for which the State is responsible, particularly its general revenues, liabilities, and assets (and particularly operations related to major public–private partnerships). However, until now, this entity is not yet a reality (Court of Auditors, 2017), which makes it difficult to have the financial reporting statements of the government as a whole.

Overall, considering prior studies developed in the Portuguese context, one can affirm that information preparers, standard setters, and auditors in general appreciate the advantages of the new accounting system of SNC-AP because of improvements in the transparency and quality of financial reporting and homogenization of criteria with business entities' accounting. However, there are also some difficulties related to the training of human resources, information systems and its communication with the central platform, and the involvement of politicians and public entities' senior management in the process of change.

Therefore, given that Portugal remains at the initial phase of the process toward IPSAS adoption, it is expected that some criticalities and difficulties are identified by accounting practitioners and auditors. Standard setters are more optimistic about the evolution of the process but still acknowledge that more support and training are needed. However, it is important to understand the particular situation of Portugal in the general context of European countries where these changes are happening. IPSAS implementation is not yet a consensual point in the literature, and some EU countries (e.g., Germany and Finland) are not yet convinced about their advantages. Prior studies have found a great heterogeneity in the adoption of IPSAS among different countries (Christiaens, Reyniers, & Rollé, 2010; Christiaens, Vanhee, Manes-Rossi, Aversano, & Van Cauwenberge, 2015; EUROSTAT, 2012). Moreover, literature has shown limited evidence on the efficiency of accrual-based accounting systems in public sector organizations (Arnaboldi & Lapsley, 2009; Lapsley, Mussari, & Paulsson, 2009).

Consequently, despite the particularities of the Portuguese context (such as bureaucracy and the excessive centralized and legalistic system) that can undermine the process of public sector accounting changes, the difficulties encountered by practitioners can also be explained by those identified by scholars with a critical perspective on IPSAS adoption. An important issue is that accrual-based IPSAS is not mandatory. Thus, IPSAS adoption depends on free choice (motivated by instrumental and rational reasons) or institutional pressures (motivated by the influence and pressures of outside parties and the need to legitimate internal actions). In Portugal, institutional pressures have played a key role in the reform (Gomes et al., 2015), and sometimes these institutional pressures are not aligned with the internal strategy to implement changes. However, since the reform is still in its early days, it is rather premature to study its effects. Further studies should be developed to better understand the changes in practice.

References

Araújo, J. (2001). Improving public service delivery: The crossroads between NPM and traditional bureaucracy. *Public Administration, 79*(4), 915–932.

Araújo, J. (2002). NPM and the change in Portuguese central government. *International Public Management Journal, 5*(3), 223–236.

Araújo, J., & Branco, J. (2009). Implementing performance based management in the traditional bureaucracy of Portugal. *Public Administration, 87*(3), 557–573.

Arnaboldi, M., & Lapsley, I. (2009). On the implementation of accrual accounting: A study of conflict and ambiguity. *European Accounting Review, 18*(4), 809–836.

Brusca, I., & Condor, V. (2002). Towards the harmonisation of local accounting systems in the international context. *Financial Accountability & Management, 18*(2), 129–162.

Christiaens, J., Reyniers, B., & Rollé, C. (2010). Impact of IPSAS on reforming governmental financial information systems: A comparative study. *International Review of Administrative Sciences, 76*(3), 537–554.

Christiaens, J., Vanhee, C., Manes-Rossi, F., Aversano, N., & Van Cauwenberge, P. (2015). The effects of IPSAS on reforming governmental financial reporting: An international comparison. *International Review of Administrative Sciences, 81*(1), 158–177.

Court of Auditors. (2016). *Audit to the SNC-AP implementation – Interim Report I. Audit Report No. 13/2016, 2nd Section.* Portugal: Court of Auditors. Retrieved from http://www.tcontas.pt/pt/actos/rel_auditoria/2016/2s/rel013-2016-2s.pdf

Court of Auditors. (2017). *Audit to the SNC-AP implementation – Interim Report II. Audit Report No. 6/2017, 2nd Section,* Portugal: Court of Auditors. Retrieved from https://www.tcontas.pt/pt/actos/rel_auditoria/2017/2s/rel006-2017-2s.shtm

ESA. (2010). *European system of accounts.* European Comission. Available at https://ec.europa.eu/eurostat/documents/3859598/5925693/KS-02-13-269-EN.PDF/44cd9d01-bc64-40e5-bd40-d17df0c69334.

EUROSTAT. (2012). *Overview and comparison of public accounting and auditing practices in the 27 EU Member States.* Retrieved Janeiro 2015, from European Commission website: http://ec.europa.eu/eurostat/documents/1015035/4261806/study-on-public-accounting-andauditing-2012.pdf/5ad43e2b-2ba7-4b05-afab-d690fc2ad9dd

Ferreira, L., & Sarmento, M. (2009). Investigação quantitativa em contabilidade: investigação por inquérito. In M. J. Major & R. Vieira (Eds.), *Contabilidade e Controlo de Gestão: Teoria, Metodologia e Prática.* Lisboa, Portugal: Escolar Editora.

Gomes, P., Brusca, I., & Fernandes, M. J. (2019). Implementing the International Public Sector Accounting Standards for consolidated financial statements: Facilitators, benefits and challenges. *Public Money & Management, 39*(8), 544–552.

Gomes, P., Brusca, I., Fernandes, M. J., & Montesinos, V. (2018). The challenge of implementing the IPSAS: The experience of Portugal and Spain. *X International EIASM Public Sector Conference.* Lund University, Lund, Sweden.

Gomes, P., Fernandes, M. J., & Carvalho, J. (2015). The international harmonization process of public sector accounting in Portugal: The perspective of different stakeholders. *International Journal of Public Administration, 38*(4), 268–281.

Gomes, P., & Mendes, S. (2013). Performance measurement and management in Portuguese law enforcement. *Public Money and Management, 33*(1), 31–38.

Hill, M. M., & Hill, A. (2008). *Investigação por Questionário (2ª Edição).* Lisboa, Portugal: Edições Sílabo.

IFAC. (2018). Handbook of International Public Sector Accounting Pronouncements, edited by International Federation of Accountants (volume I), IFAC, USA. Available online at https://www.ifac.org/system/files/publications/files/IPSASB-HandBook-2018-Volume-1.pdf.

Jorge, S. (2015). Public sector accounting and auditing in Portugal. In I. Brusca, E. Caperchione, S. Cohen, & F. Manes Rossi (Eds.), *Public sector accounting and auditing in Europe – The challenge of harmonization* (Chapter 11, pp. 173–190). Hampshire: Palgrave Macmillan. ISBN: 978-1-349-69007-7.

Jorge, S., Brusca, I., & Nogueira, S. P. (2019). Translating IPSAS into National Standards: An illustrative comparison between Spain and Portugal. *Journal of Comparative Policy Analysis: Research and Practice, 21*(5), 445–462.

Jorge, S., Carvalho, J., & Fernandes, M. J. (2008). From cash to accruals in Portuguese local government accounting: What has truly changed. *Tékhne, 6*(10), 239–261.

Lapsley, I., Mussari, R., & Paulsson, G. (2009). On the adoption of accrual accounting in the public sector: A self-evident and problematic reform. *European Accounting Review, 18*(4), 719–723.

McLeod, R. H., & Harun, H. (2014). Public sector accounting reform at local government level in Indonesia. *Financial Accountability & Management, 30*(2), 238–258.

Nogueira, S., Jorge, S., & Ribeiro, N. (2020). The institutionalization of public sector accounting reforms: The role of pilot entities. *Journal of Public Budgeting, Accounting and Financial Management.* Ahead of print.

Ridder, H.-G., Bruns, H.-J., & Spier, F. (2005). Analysis of public management change process: The case of local government accounting reforms in Germany. *Public Administration, 83*(2), 443–471.

CHAPTER 4

The Application of the IPSAS in Spain

Isabel Brusca, Rosa María Dasí, Amparo Gimeno-Ruiz, and Vicente Montesinos

Abstract Governmental accounting was adapted to IPSAS in Spain in 2010, following the reform in the business accounting system to adapt it to IFRS. However, the budget maintains the modified cash criteria and there is an integrated system that includes financial and budgeting accounting. This chapter analyses the normative process and the main challenges and benefits that the new system has had at the three levels of government: central, regional, and local. In order to understand the experience of practitioners, a survey for accountants and financial directors has been carried

I. Brusca (✉)
Department of Accounting and Finance, University of Zaragoza, Zaragoza, Spain
e-mail: ibrusca@unizar.es

R. M. Dasí • A. Gimeno-Ruiz • V. Montesinos
Department of Accounting, University of Valencia, Valencia, Spain
e-mail: rosa.m.dasi@uv.es; amparo.gimeno@uv.es; Vicente.Montesinos@uv.es

I. Brusca et al. (eds.), *Challenges in the Adoption of International Public Sector Accounting Standards*, Public Sector Financial Management, https://doi.org/10.1007/978-3-030-63125-3_4

out at each government level. The results show that budgetary reporting is considered still more useful than accrual financial statements, due fundamentally to the role that the laws give to this information.

Keywords Accrual accounting • Budget • Governmental accounting • IPSAS • Spain

4.1 Description of the Normative Process of Governmental Accounting in Spain

Spain is a parliamentary monarchy that was integrated into the European Union in 1986. According to the 1978 Constitution, its public administration is organized on three levels: national or central government, regional governments, and local governments. The central government level is the most important with respect to the size of its expenditure in the gross domestic product.

Since the 1990s, efforts to reform public management have been intense, driven by the international trend of adapting it to New Public Management principles. The three levels of governments have carried out reform measures with the intention of improving the efficiency of resources, imitating Anglo-Saxon countries. In accordance with Pollitt and Bouckaert (2017), taking into account the reforms implemented in the country, Spain could be included in the Neo-Weberian State group, with a reaffirmation of the role of the state. At the same time, performance management philosophy has been introduced into the elaboration and management of the budget (Ballart & Zapico, 2010).

These reforms included public sector accounting, and accrual accounting was implemented in central government in 1986 and in local government in 1992. As in many continental European countries, the accounting system in Spain corresponds to an administrative law model, so accounting standards are set through laws or decrees, whose application is compulsory, approved by the government. The Ministry of Economy has the responsibility for elaborating accounting standards for the business sector, which are drawn up by the Spanish Institute of Accounting and Auditing (Instituto de Contabilidad y Auditoría de Cuentas, ICAC), a dependent entity of the Ministry. For the public sector, the Ministry of Finance sets accounting standards through a specific body, the Government Comptroller's Office (Intervención General de la Administración del

Estado, IGAE). There is a specific department of accounting standards, inside the IGAE, which is responsible for the development of accounting standards for central and local government levels. Parliament approves accounting legislation that provides, as a general legal framework, the accounting principles and standards to be applied for financial reporting purposes.

As in other European countries with a continental legal tradition, the influence of the accounting profession is very weak, unlike other countries where a "common law" tradition leads to a strong influence of the accounting profession (Montesinos, Pina, Torres, & Vela, 1998). Accounting standards are set by law and are compulsory.

The accounting reforms in the Spanish public sector have pursued, as one of their fundamental objectives, the harmonization of the applicable accounting standards in the three levels of government (central, regional, and local) following a vertical model (top-down approach) for the standardization of governmental accounting, transferring the reforms implemented at the central level to the other two levels of the administration. Nevertheless, the Ministry of Economy is only responsible for the accounting standards of central and local government. As a consequence, accounting standards are uniform and homogeneous in these two levels of government, and also the legal framework of finance and budgeting. The regional governments have autonomy, which implies that they have legislative power. This autonomy and legislative power includes accounting, budgeting, and auditing aspects. There is, however, a Common Financial Law of Regional Governments. Furthermore, regional governments have progressively adapted their accounting regulations to those issued by IGAE.

There is a long tradition of developing Accounting Plans, both for business and public sectors. There is a General Governmental Accounting Plan (GGAP-Plan General de Contabilidad Pública) that serves as a framework for all the entities in the public sector. Following this general standard, adaptations are issued for the different governmental levels: central, regional, and local.

The GGAP contains the accounting principles and specific standards to be applied and provides a description of the bookkeeping rules, as well as the models of financial statements to be prepared on an annual basis. The Spanish government accounting system has always been based on the business accounting model, although it includes adaptations for the public sector.

Regulation 2002/1606/EC of the European Parliament and of the Council of 19 July 2002 requires the application of International Financial Reporting Standards (IFRS) to the consolidated statements of quoted groups, which led to a debate about the advisability of adapting the Spanish system to the International Standards, with the aim of avoiding differences in accounting standards between individual and consolidated accounts. The outcome was a new Accounting Plan for business, approved in November 2007 and applicable as of 1 January 2008. This new Plan was adapted to the IFRS with the intention of homogenizing both between listed and unlisted companies and between individual and group accounts.

The reform in the private sector was followed by another in the public sector and in 2010 a new GGAP was approved, which is adapted to business standards and to the IPSAS. This is the general framework, but adaptations of this GGAP were passed for central government (2011) and for local governments (2013). The competence to set the accounting standards of governmental entities in the case of regional governments (autonomous communities) corresponds to the communities themselves, and they approve their respective standards adapted to the GGAP framework.

In relation to these processes, it is noteworthy that IPSAS are used as a basic reference, but do not replace the Spanish Accounting Plan, as in many other countries that have established similar standards.

In spite of the adoption of accrual accounting into the public sector and the more recent adaptation to international standards, there have been no reforms in the budgetary criteria, which maintain the modified cash basis of accounting. Thus, the accounting system is split into two, one for accounting information and the other for budgetary reporting, but coordinated into the same software application. The budgetary system still dominates in the control and management of governments, as it is approved by the legislative power and contains the rules for the management of the resources, so that political debate is focused on it. This leads to a higher use of budgetary reporting than accrual financial statements (Brusca & Montesinos, 2013) due to the legal-administrative culture and the role given by law to budgetary information, as in many other continental countries (Cohen, Manes Rossi, Caperchione, & Brusca, 2019; Van Helden & Reichard, 2018).

4.2 The Central Government Experience

The Spanish Central Government introduced accrual financial statements in 1986, so it can be considered a pioneer, in line with Anglo-Saxon countries. Since then, there have been two important reforms of the system: in 1996 and 2011. These reforms have always followed those in the business sector because of European Union requirements for adapting the Spanish system, first to European directives and later to the International Financial Reporting Standards. In this sense, the evolution of public sector accounting has been marked by the evolution of the business sector, implying an approach to the IPSAS. Another important consequence of the mimetic to the business sector has been the introduction of consolidated financial statements in 2015.

The accounting standards approved in 2011 for central government had two aims: (a) adapting public sector accounting standards to business accounting standards, as this was the path that has always guided public accounting reforms; and (b) adapting accounting standards to IPSAS.

4.2.1 *The Adaptation to IPSAS: Main Changes in the Accounting System*

The 2011 reform has led to many important changes in the financial reporting system, including the introduction of a conceptual framework, changes in the valuation criteria, and the introduction of new financial statements.

The Conceptual Framework of the General Governmental Accounting Plan

The conceptual framework defines the concepts and fundamental principles that guide the recognition and measurement of the elements of the financial statements. It took as its references the conceptual framework for the business sector (based on that of IPSASB); the preface to the IPSAS elaborated by the IPSASB and the definitions of IPSAS 1 "Presentation of Financial Statements." The conceptual framework of the IPSASB had not been issued when the GGAP was approved.

The conceptual framework defines two objectives of the accounting information: to provide useful information for government decision making and for accountability purposes. In accordance with the IPSAS 1 and IPSAS 24, the financial statements introduced to achieve these objectives are balance sheet, statement of financial performance, cash flow statement, statement of changes in net assets/equity, budgetary execution statement, and notes to the financial statements.

The characteristics of the accounting information are the same as those contained in the IASB conceptual framework and IPSAS 1: *understandability*, *relevance*, *reliability*, and *comparability*. In IPSAS 1, both *neutrality* and *prudence* are identified as components of *reliability*. In the Spanish GGAP, prudence is contained within the accounting principles with the intention of achieving homogeneity with the private sector Accounting Plan.

With respect to the accounting principles, due to the duality of the system, they are divided into two groups: those applicable to the accrual accounting statements and those for budgetary statements.

The elements of the financial statements are also defined in the conceptual framework. Assets are defined as goods, rights, and other economic resources controlled by the entity resulting from past events from which it is probable that the entity can obtain economic performance or service potential in the future. As a consequence, assets are classified into two types:

- Assets that generate future economic returns, including those that can be used for the provision of goods or services. This type of assets is similar to the assets of the business sector.
- Assets that generate service potential, including those that have a purpose other than to generate a commercial return, such as social economic flows generated by these assets that benefit the community, that is, their social benefits or service potential.

An important implication of the definition of the concept of asset is that infrastructure and property assets for general use are included in it, while they were not considered as assets in the previous General Accounting Plan. These assets were written off the balance sheet when they began to be used. The new regulation is in line with IPSAS 17, that states that infrastructure assets should meet the definition of property, plant, and equipment and should be accounted for in the balance sheet.

The Valuation Criteria

Adapting government accounting to the IPSAS also introduced some changes in the valuation criteria for assets, debts, expenses, and income. In particular, the GGAP introduced fair value, which is used to measure certain assets and liabilities. The GGAP allows the use of fair value for valuing assets, subsequent to their acquisition when their fair value can be measured reliably. This is in line with the revaluation model included in IPSAS 17, but it is necessary for the IGAE to approve its use. In this respect, the public sector differs from the business regulation, where fair value is only used for financial instruments.

As for the impairment of the assets, the standard differentiates between assets that generate future economic returns and those that generate service potential. The cost of replacement is used to assess the impairment of assets that generate service potential.

The regulation of intangible assets is similar to IPSAS 31, although there are some differences for investigation expenditures, which can be recognized as assets if certain characteristics are presented.

The application of the new system adapted to the IPSAS in central government led to improvements in the quality of financial reporting and was the initial step toward the elaboration of consolidated statements. An important innovation in central government, derived from the application of the IPSAS, has been the implementation of consolidated financial statements. In 2013 the standard for the elaboration of consolidated statements in the public sector was approved and it has been compulsory for central government since 2014. The standards were elaborated taking as a reference IPSAS 6 to 8, which have been later replaced by IPSAS 35 to 37.

A regulation of 2015 (Order HAP/1724/2015, regulating the preparation of the Central Government Financial Report) defines the process for the implementation of consolidated reporting standards in central government, with a gradual process starting for the 2014 financial statements. Given the number of entities to be integrated and the high number of internal operations, the Order establishes a transitional period in which, in certain cases, the equity method could be used until 2016 for some dependent entities, updating the value of the investment in the entity to the percentage of participation in its equity, without prior homogenization or elimination of results from internal operations. The first consolidated financial statements applying the full consolidation method for dependent entities were those of the financial report of 2017.

Table 4.1 summarizes the IPSAS that have been taken into consideration in the central government accounting standards.

Table 4.1 IPSAS considered in the Spanish Central Government Accounting regulation

IPSAS	*Year issued*
IPSAS 1—Presentation of Financial Statements	2000
IPSAS 2—Cash Flow Statements	2000
IPSAS 3—Accounting Policies, Changes in Accounting Estimates and Errors	2000
IPSAS 4—The Effects of Changes in Foreign Exchange Rates	2000
IPSAS 5—Borrowing Costs	2000
IPSAS 6—Consolidated and Separate Financial Statements (introduced in the standards for consolidated statements)	2000
IPSAS 7—Investments in Associates (introduced in the standards for consolidated statements)	2000
IPSAS 8—Interests in Joint Ventures (introduced in the standards for consolidated statements)	2000
IPSAS 9—Revenue from Exchange Transactions	2001
IPSAS 12—Inventories	2001
IPSAS 13—Leases	2001
IPSAS 14—Events after the Reporting Date	2001
IPSAS 15—Financial Instruments: Disclosure and Presentation	2001
IPSAS 16—Investment Property	2001
IPSAS 17—Property, Plant, and Equipment	2001
IPSAS 19—Provisions, Contingent Liabilities, and Contingent Assets	2002
IPSAS 20—Related Party Disclosures	2002
IPSAS 21—Impairment of Non-Cash-Generating Assets	2004
IPSAS 23—Revenue from Non-Exchange Transactions (Taxes and Transfers)	2006
IPSAS 24—Presentation of Budget Information in Financial Statements	2008
IPSAS 26—Impairment of Cash-Generating Assets	2006
IPSAS 27—Financial Instruments: Presentation	2010
IPSAS 28—Financial Instruments: Recognition and Measurement	2010
IPSAS 29—Financial Instruments: Disclosures	2010

4.2.2 *The Adaptation to IPSAS: Impact in the Financial Statements*

The first financial statements of the central government applying the IPSAS were those of 2011 and due to the changes explained before, some adjustments were required in the data of 2010. As a consequence, the data of 2010 and 2011 were not comparable and the financial statements of 2011 only contained the data of that year. Among the necessary adjustments, it is worth mentioning the incorporation of heritage assets in the central administration financial reports. As a result of the application of these new criteria, an increase in the net assets/equity of 30,246 million euros in the net worth took place, going from -280,797 million euros in 2010 to -265,551 million euros in 2011.

It should also be noted that the IGAE decided not to apply the model of revaluation of fixed assets. There were also exceptions in the application of the effective interest rate on the national debt for the first year. This indicates the difficulties of implementing these two criteria at central government level and that the criterion of fair value for assets may not be necessary.

The elaboration of the statement of changes in net assets/equity and the cash flow statement was another novelty introduced in 2011, as a consequence of the application of the IPSAS.

Another important effect of the IPSAS application was the elaboration of consolidated statements for the central government in 2014. Until then, an aggregated financial report was elaborated, in which the entities were only aggregated. The consolidated statement included a total of 382 dependent entities (out of 396), 317 of them using the full consolidation method and the others with the equity method. In 2017, the financial statements were elaborated using the full method of consolidation for all the dependent entities. This has been considered one of the most important advantages of the application of the IPSAS.

4.2.3 The Opinion of the Practitioners: Preparers and Auditors

The Opinion of Preparers

As the adoption of the new standards has had an important impact on the financial statements, we have carried out an interview with two accountants of the Treasury with the aim of showing what their experience has been. The two interviewees have a long experience in public sector accounting and have been working in the Treasury for more than 20 years. The opinions of both of them are quite similar about the new system: both consider that it is more adequate than the old one and that the new model fits the characteristics of Spanish central government well and that the new criteria are adequate for the public sector, although they are aware that the application of fair value may involve some difficulties, especially when there is no market value for assets.

They also consider that the main advantage of the new system is that different entities across the public sector (administrative organisms, business and nonprofit entities, such as foundations) have a homogeneous system and consolidated statements can be elaborated easier. In fact, consolidated statements are produced since 2015 (first financial statements correspond to 2014) , as a response to a Motion of the Court of Auditors of 2005 on the procedures of formation, scope, and content of the General Account of the State, in which it was considered that it presented deficiencies, preventing the fulfillment of their objectives, advocating for the formation of a single account.

Other benefits of the system in the opinion of both interviewees are: increasing the comparability among entities, increasing the quality of financial reporting, increasing the accountability and transparency of local government and the control of government actions. In fact, the consolidated financial statements of 2015 mention that the application of international standards leads to improvements in the quality of financial reporting, allowing the elaboration of consolidated financial statements.

However, it seems that the new standards have not introduced changes in the use of the information for strategic planning and decision making. In fact, when we asked these accountants about the uses of the information, they answered that the information is mainly used for accountability so that the central government can inform citizens and the Supreme Audit Institution.

As for the usefulness of the information, the accountants still value budgetary reporting more than accrual financial reporting. They also consider that the cash flow statement is very useful. However, the statement of financial performance and the statement of changes in net assets/equity are not very appreciated. This shows that the new standards are limited in the introduction of new useful information in spite of the new financial statements.

The level of use of the information is low in the following aims: decision making, strategic decision about public policies, management control, performance measurement and evaluation, elaboration of the budget.

Consolidated financial statements also have a limited usefulness; the two interviewees consider that their main usefulness is accountability of the activities of the whole government. This information is also considered useful to determine the total assets and debts of the group of entities, as well as its revenues and expenses. However, they do not consider that the information is useful for taking decisions about different management forms of public services and the number of dependent entities that must be maintained, bearing in mind that dependent entities have increased in recent years.

Conceptual statements and studies issued by accounting standards board, such as the IPSASB (2018) and GASB (1987), contain a long list of users of financial statements, such as creditors and investors, resource providers, management, citizens, taxpayers and voters, and oversight bodies. Aiming to test if these are also users of financial reporting in the practice, we have asked the two interviewees about their opinion from the perspective of central government. Both consider that the main users are oversight and control bodies, such as the Supreme Audit Institution and internal control bodies. Also the political parties in the opposition use the information with political aims, trying to criticize government policies. However, it can be highlighted that financial entities are not considered important users of financial statements, in spite that they give loans and financial resources to central government. Neither the citizens nor the taxpayers are considered important users of financial statements.

The main challenges to guarantee a successful implementation of the new standard have been invest in human resources training, new information and software system, involving top management in the process of change, and obtaining political compromise in the implementation of the reform.

The main obstacles to the new system have been resistance to change, excessive bureaucracy in the process and the technical difficulties in the new system.

This evidences that in order to guarantee the application of the EPSAS, the European Commission first needs to create a positive environment for its adoption in member countries by obtaining the commitment of the politicians of the countries, the resources for training civil servants, and the software for the governments.

The Opinion of Auditors

Regarding the opinion of the auditors, we have collected the responses of eight auditors with high responsibility and long experience in the Spanish Court of Auditors, with training in Economics, Business Administration and Law, who have responded to a questionnaire previously submitted. There is gender parity among the respondents, and except in one case, none of the experts studied public accounting during their university studies.

The questionnaire asks for the assessment of 1 to 5 of various questions,[1] grouped into eight blocks of questions, related to the following aspects:

a) Suitability of the new accounting system derived from the GGAP adapted to IPSAS
b) Advantages or benefits of the new accounting system
c) Difficulties or obstacles to the adoption of the new system
d) Measures to be taken to guarantee the success of the governmental accounting reform
e) Usefulness of information for decision making
f) Usefulness of the various types of information produced for specific purposes
g) The use of financial statements by the different categories of users
h) Usefulness of consolidated financial statements

a) Suitability of the new accounting system derived from the GGAP adapted to IPSAS

In this block of the questionnaire, the auditors are requested to indicate to what extent the new accounting information system seems appropriate, in relation to the aspects mentioned below.

Seven of the eight experts think that the application of fair value is appropriate, placing its valuation in the two highest tranches of convenience, considering also that, by establishing a homogeneous system with companies, accounts consolidation is facilitated (six of the answers are located in the two highest sections of conformity).

Half of the experts consider the new system very adequate, more than the previous regulations of 2002, and the rest of the responses showing a medium or high level of conformity. Also, most of the responses consider that the new model is better suited to the context of the Spanish ceneral administration, with two responses that show a medium conformity with this assessment and one that leans toward a low conformity. In the same way, most experts estimate, with a high or very high level of conformity, that the assessment criteria are more adequate than the previous ones, and the rest of the respondents agree with this opinion, although with a medium level of conformity.

[1] 1 = null or non-existent; 2 = low; 3 = medium; 4 = high; 5 = very high

Two of the responses consider that the increase in complexity of the system is not compensated by its greater utility, a critical opinion that, although with less emphasis, four other experts also adopt (two of them consider that the adequacy of the system is low and two others they place it at a medium level). Regarding the relevance of the changes, only three responses consider them of high or very high relevance, two consider them not relevant, and the rest of medium or low relevance.

In short, a positive assessment of the reform is observed, although in some aspects the new system can be considered excessively complicated and the changes not too relevant.

b) Advantages or benefits of the new accounting system

At this point, the interviewees consider various significant aspects of high or very high relevance, such as: improving the quality of information; greater transparency of public accounts; the improvement of the accounts consolidation process; and the increase in the level of comparability of information.

The valuation of the benefits is between medium and high in relation to: improvements in accountability; control of government actions; the greater use of information for internal decision making and for internal control and planning; finally, in this range, the greater reliability of the public accounts is placed.

Although with divergences regarding the valuation of the auditors, it is considered important to achieve standardization in information disclosure: two auditors believe that it is a very high benefit; two other interviewees consider this benefit high and the same number attributes a benefit of medium relevance to this issue; one answer estimates the profit low and the last one considers it null.

Thus, we observe that experts highlight the main advantages of improving the quality of information; greater transparency of public accounts; the improvement of the consolidation process; and the increase in the level of comparability of information.

On a second level we find the improvements in accountability; control of government actions; the greater use of information for internal decision making and for internal control and planning; as well as the greater reliability of public accounts.

More divergences appear in the standardization of information disclosure, but a clear majority positively estimate the consequences that can be expected in this regard.

c) Difficulties or obstacles to the adoption of the new system

Regarding the difficulties or obstacles arising from the introduction of the new system, none of them is considered very high by the majority of respondents.

However, the existence of difficulties, high or very high, regarding the lack of training of human resources in the economic and financial area and the resistance to change are brought to light. The lack of participation of political parties is also considered a high or very high difficulty by half of the experts.

The lack of participation of senior management, the lack of culture in financial matters, the excessive bureaucracy of public administration, and the reduced knowledge of the new system are described as medium or high difficulties by most of the experts consulted.

As sources of medium or low difficulties we find the lack of technical support and the lack of appropriate information systems.

To the previous assessments, the unfavorable opinion on the usefulness of the information must be added. Thus, four of the respondents consider it as a disadvantage or difficulty of medium or low level and two other experts as an important or very relevant difficulty.

In short, even when serious difficulties are not appreciated, except for the disinterest of political parties, there are several significant obstacles related to the training of human resources, the adequacy of computer systems and technical support, resistance to change and problems of lack of financial culture, knowledge of the new system, and involvement of senior management.

d) Measures to be taken to guarantee the success of the governmental accounting reform

In this regard, respondents show unanimity in assessing the measures aimed at investing in the training of human resources, the involvement of senior management in the process of change, and the development of mechanisms for the application of reform. With a single opinion describing the action to be of medium utility, the auditors also consider of high-very high utility the provision to the entities of appropriate information systems.

Between medium (three responses), high (one response), and very high (four responses) is positioned the usefulness of obtaining political commitment to the implementation of the reform.

Finally, even though half of the respondents continue to consider the requirement of an independent audit of high or very high utility, the other 50% consider the measure to be of medium or low utility.

e) Usefulness of information for decision making

With regard to the usefulness of financial statements for decision making, there is broad agreement in the responses considering that the balance sheet and the budgetary execution statement (comparing budget and actual amounts) have a very high utility.

The statement of financial performance is considered to be of high or very high utility by five of the eight respondents, while the utility of the statement of cash flows is between the middle and very high positions, with more modest assessments for the statement of changes in net assets/equity, to which half of the respondents place it among those of high and very high profit, while the other 50% attribute it a low or medium usefulness.

Regarding the valuation of the indicators, the budgetary ones are clearly considered as of high or very high utility by seven of the respondents, followed by the financial indicators, valued as of high or very high utility by six of the experts. The usefulness of economic and efficiency indicators is valued as high or very high in half of the responses, an assessment attributed by the majority of respondents to the effectiveness indicators.

It should be noted that only in the case of the statement of financial performance its utility is evaluated with zero, in one of the responses received.

In summary, the financial statements are considered of high or very high usefulness by the majority of respondents, although in the case of the statement of changes in net assets/equity a low evaluation is given by three of the experts, compared to the rest that place it among the medium, high, or very high valuations and in the case of the statement of cash flows, to which half of the experts attribute a medium utility, in contrast to three that consider it high and one that places it in the low range.

Regarding the indicators, the best valued for their usefulness for decisions are the budgetary and financial ones, in this order, while the usefulness of economic, efficiency, and effectiveness indicators reaches more modest valuations.

f) Usefulness of the various types of information produced for specific purposes

There is unanimity of the inquired auditors in considering high or very high the usefulness of consolidated financial statements in the new system for accountability purposes. Five experts also attribute this rating to accountability with individual financial statements.

Most of the respondents rate the usefulness of the information offered in the new states for the purpose of decision making on management and service provision, the preparation of a management report, planning and management control, measurement and evaluation of this management, accountability to citizens about it, and the preparation of information on budgetary stability.

Finally, the evaluation is medium-low for the usefulness of the information for the purpose of making strategic decisions on public policies and for the budgetary process.

g) The use of financial statements by the different categories of users

If we focus our attention on the utility of the new financial statements for the different categories of users, all the answers unanimously indicate that the utility for the Court of Auditors is very high and all experts consider it high or very high in the case of comptrollers and other experts in charge of financial economic management (only one response assesses benefit as high and the rest as very high).

The utility of the statements for the members of the delegated commissions of the government is considered medium-high in the majority of the answers, although, in the rest of the valuations, in one case a low utility is attributed and a null utility in two other responses.

The majority of the respondents consider the utility of the financial statements for the members of the government to be null or low, although two of the responses consider it high and one of medium utility. Also, most of the responses consider the utility of the financial statements to citizens to be of little or null utility and only two place it in a medium range.

Most of the answers set the usefulness of these statements for the political groups of the government and the opposition in a medium or low utility range, with a high utility evaluation for the government group in a response and another one that considers this information of very high utility for opposition groups.

In global terms, the survey shows that experts consider the information presented in the financial statements and the indicators contemplated in the reform to be useful for decision making, with a clear gradation that places budget information first, followed by the statement of financial position.

The majority of respondents consider the new accounting system adequate, with reservations about the justification, in terms of utility, of the greater complexity of the system.

With regard to the advantages, the opinions that consider them low or non-existent are not significant, with a majority of the responses located in a moderate range between medium and high benefits, recognizing in some cases a very high advantage.

The main difficulties are related to the lack of training of human resources, the low involvement of politicians and senior management, and the resistance to change. In no case do the answers indicate that the problems or difficulties are non-existent, but they are not generally considered as excessively serious obstacles.

The opinions on the usefulness of the information produced are diverse, although a very positive assessment can be found for the purpose of accountability, both with individual and consolidated statements. High utility is also recognized for preparing information on budgetary stability and there is a certain skepticism about its usefulness for other uses, as in the case of strategic decisions on public policies.

There is practical unanimity regarding the necessary or important measures to guarantee the success of the reform, among which are the human resources training, the involvement of senior management, and the development of adequate information systems.

It is considered that the consolidated financial statements have a special utility to know the debt of the public group, as well as all its expenses and income and for an adequate accountability.

Finally, among the users most benefited by the new system, the Court of Auditors, the comptrollers, and other experts in charge of management stand out, leaving the citizens as a whole lagging behind in this regard.

h) Usefulness of consolidated financial statements

Seven of the eight respondents consider the utility of the consolidated financial statements to know the debt of the entire group constituted by the General State Administration high or very high, and only in the remaining case is this assessment lowered to the level of medium benefit. The majority of experts also consider that the consolidated statements have high or very high utility to know all the expenses and income of the group (two consider it medium level), and that same evaluation is attributed by the majority for the purpose of accountability of all the group activities (only two experts consider a medium utility and one of the respondents does not see any utility for this purpose).

The majority of the respondents place the utility of the consolidated statements for the purpose of making decisions on the creation or dissolution of dependent entities at the other extreme (50% attribute a null profit, two low, and two medium) and identical valuations correspond to the usefulness for decision making on the most adequate form of service provision.

Finally, the majority of responses place the valuations of the usefulness of the consolidated information to determine the budgetary stability of all the entities of the group in the medium-high range, whereas three consider it without utility or with a low utility.

4.3 Regional Governments: The Heterogeneous Situation Inside the Country

4.3.1 Accounting in Regional Governments: Political Context and Reform Guidelines

Currently, 17 autonomous communities exist and were constituted between 1979 and 1983. There are also two autonomous cities (Ceuta y Melilla). Each of them has its own government and parliament and, unlike other countries, in Spain each autonomous community has its own competences, which very often differ from one autonomous community to another.

Accounting standards for business enterprises are the same in the whole country. However, in the case of public sector accounting, GGAP is a general framework that has to be adapted to central, regional, and local governments.

The adaptation of these standards by regional governments or autonomous communities has not only taken a considerable delay, but in most of them, the adapted rules either have been passed recently or are still pending. In fact, only 12 of the 17 autonomous communities have adapted their accounting regulations to the GGAP-2010, of which 8 have done so in the last two years. The fact of linking the program for the application of the Autonomous Liquidity Fund *(FLA)* to the accounting reform seems to have accelerated the process. *The FLA,* created by Royal Decree-law 21/2012, of July 13, is a mechanism to support the liquidity of the autonomous communities, of a temporary nature and voluntary, which allows meeting the financial needs of the communities, while the difficulties of access to the financial markets persist. One of the conditions for accessing these aid funds is to carry out the adaptation to the GGAP-2010.

4.3.2 Some Key Issues About the Autonomous Communities Accounting Reform

After analyzing the recent developments of governmental accounting in Spain, and taking as a reference the study of Dasí, Montesinos, and Vela (2018), our aim is to present several key questions that generally arise both in academic and professional debates in the field of autonomous communities accounting:

1. The complexity of the accounting system and the relationship between budgetary and financial accounting information.
2. The scope and content of financial standardized reports (annual financial statements).
3. Consolidated financial statements.
4. The reporting of information related to national accounting figures.

The ***relationship between budgetary and financial accounting information*** in Spanish governmental accounting systems, at all levels of government, has always been carried out through the link of both types of information within a single accounting and reporting system.

The key question that arises is if the detail and volume of information required with respect to these two areas are truly useful, considering the information needs of the different types of users. Some groups of users such as politicians, journalists, or taxpayers have traditionally criticized the complexity of the accounting system. They consider that the volume of financial information required is too high taking into account its further use for the decision-making process in governments, basically based on the handling of budgetary information. In that sense, the study of Brusca and Montesinos (2013) show that "after two decades of reforms in financial and management systems, financial directors still consider that budgetary reporting is the most useful, basically because the control of expenditure is still based on the budget."

As noted in the PwC report (2017), given the different objectives between budgetary and financial accounting, some governments make a distinction between the two accounting systems. Indeed, budgetary accounting may require data capture at a different level (scope difference) and at a different time (timing difference). However, despite the apparent distinction between the two, the IMF (2017) recommends having a common and integrated account coding structure for both budgetary and financial accounting. Budget and accounting classifications must be developed together to ensure that they are coherent with each other.

The fact is that in the social and political environment of Spanish public sector accounting, the preferential use of budgetary information is clearly generalized among the different users of accounting information, who have always considered the information of the budget to be more relevant than the one presented in the framework of financial accounting.

The *scope and content of annual financial statements* is another key issue that is worth to analyze, especially considering that their form and content are clearly influenced by business accounting.

The existing IPSAS do not foresee a standard chart of accounts. IPSAS 1 includes some minimal presentation requirements relating to the statement of financial position and statement of financial performance, however it does not impose how to meet these requirements via the use of specific accounts. Then, national governments are free to design a chart of accounts as well as reporting formats that meet local and management reporting requirements (PwC, 2017).

An interesting debate can be raised about the usefulness of these reports for the users of the accounting information, especially considering that, as commented before, the majority of them usually emphasize the usefulness of the budgetary statements compared to the rest.

The development and the reporting of *consolidated annual financial statements* are an additional key question that the reform has enforced. Through our survey, we have also requested autonomous government accountants' opinion about their suitability.

The reporting of accounting information related to national accounting figures is an additional key issue considered.

As pointed out by Dasí, Montesinos, and Murgui (2016), greater comparability of financial, budgetary, and aggregated statistical reports can improve social, political, and economic decision making and accountability.

After the introduction of the 2/2012 Organic Law on Budget Stability and Financial Sustainability, Spanish local and autonomous authorities have to present additional information to the Ministry of Finance related to budget stability goals, in order to present relevant and reliable information to allow the calculation of national accounting figures according to SEC requirements. This Law has introduced a wide set of information requirements on budget stability that municipalities have to respect, as well as the preventive and disciplinary provisions therein.

Once the Ministry of Finance has processed the information and national accounting figures for autonomous (regional) government level have been calculated, we think it would be useful to include some notes to financial statements reporting the results obtained, in national accounting terms, specially concerning debt and deficit figures. Even if this information is available for citizens from Ministry of Finance statistical base, in our survey, we have also requested autonomous government accountants' opinion on that sense.

4.3.3 Methodological Issues

In order to reveal the experiences of practitioners in regional government, a survey was designed and carried out for Spanish autonomous communities.

The design and elaboration of the survey has been based on the literature review and documentary analysis of the standards and regulation in Spain.

This questionnaire was sent to the financial directors of the 17 Spanish regional governments (autonomous communities), the complete universe. It was not sent to the autonomous cities of Ceuta and Melilla because they follow local regulations. The survey was sent by email in early-2019. Afterwards, we sent reminders in February and March and, in some cases, we contacted by phone with some of them, in order to get responses from the complete universe. Finally, we obtained the responses from 16 out of the 17 communities (response rate of 94.11%).

The questionnaire was composed of 17 questions, five of them addressed to characterize the statistical unit and the respondent who provides the answers. Depending on the interest of the measured items, two Likert scales have been established, one from 1 to 3 being 2 the neutral value and another from 1 to 5 in which 3 marks the neutral value; in both 1 represents the minimum value and the 3/5 the maximum.

It should also be noted that the level of response obtained has not been the same in all the questions, because not all the interviewees have answered all the questions.

4.3.4 *Analysis of Results*

As we have highlighted in the first part of the study, the reform of regional public accounting and its adaptation to the GGAP have taken a considerable delay. According to respondents, this delay is due, mainly, to the lack of means and technical support, followed by the lack of political interest and participation, as well as the excessive bureaucracy in public administration. The respondents give less weight to factors such as the training level of the staff in the economic-financial area or to the consideration that the provided information according to the new regulations has a low usefulness. Considering the information requirements of the new regulation, questions related to the complexity of the new accounting information system were included in the questionnaire (question number 3). The information that must be elaborated with the new regulation is considered very complex compared with its usefulness for 6 of the interviewees, and of moderate complexity for nine of them. This assessment about the complexity of the accounting information system introduced by the GGAP contrasts with the opinion of the local governmental accountants regarding the local public accounting regulations that came into force in 2015. Thus, according to Dasí, Gimeno, and Vela (2018), 55.6% of the local government accountants considered the accounting information system complex, while 43.6% deemed it as very complex. This different assessment between these two groups could be due to a better training of human resources in economic and financial issues at regional than at local level.

Regional accountants were also asked about their opinion on the suitability and/or opportunity of some issues included in the GGAP-2010 compared to those included in the previous regulations.

Regarding the application of the GGAP, a large majority (11/16) of the respondents consider that its application will facilitate the consolidation of accounts, because it establishes a system homogeneous with the business one, giving to this item a score between 4 and 5. In the other extreme, with lower scores, only two interviewees disagree.

Regarding the appropriateness of the measurement criteria introduced by the GGAP, 50% of respondents consider them more appropriate than the ones included in previous regulations. About the adequacy of application of the fair value criterion to the public sphere, a lower degree of consensus is obtained. Half of the respondents (8/16) are in a neutral position, and only five of them consider it adequate or very adequate.

On the other hand, as the European Commission (2013) points out, IPSAS are important to allow more informative and transparent financial reports of public sector entities and governments. In this sense, most of the respondents consider that the GGAP is better adapted to the regional environment than the previous regulations and they estimate that these new standards would improve accountability.

Regarding the usefulness for the decision making of the accounting information elaborated under the new regulations, 15 of the 16 regional governmental accountants consider useful or very useful the information provided by budgetary accounting, being much lower the assessment given to the information which is obtained from financial accounting. Thus, seven respondents give an intermediate weight (value 3), and only three of the respondents consider it very useful.

The trend to give less relevance to financial information than to budgetary information does not seem to have changed over the years. Thus, the studies by Montesinos, Vela, and Benito (2001) and Brusca and Montesinos (2013) also showed that those in charge of preparing accounting information at the regional and local levels considered budgetary information as the most relevant. The same behavior is observed in the Spanish local dministration (Dasí, Gimeno, & Vela, 2018).

The International Federation of Accountants (IFAC, 2014) has highlighted the importance of financial statements to assess the sustainability of organizations, considering that they are basic for understanding the financial situation of any entity. More specifically, IFAC (2012) recognizes that the statement of financial performance provides a very useful information in order to assess the ability of governments to continue providing the same services while maintaining their quality, which is one of the cornerstones of financial sustainability. The IPSAS No. 1 (IFAC, 2014) establishes that this statement reflects all the expenses and revenues that have been incurred during the year, recognized according to the accrual principle.

In relation with financial statements included in the GGAP, 66.7% of the regional governmental accountants would eliminate some of them. The statement of changes in net assets/equity and the cash flow statement are the ones which would be eliminated by the interviewees. None of the respondents indicated the budgetary statements as dispensable, which is consistent with the aforementioned evaluations, since the budgetary information is considered as the most useful. These responses are in line with the opinion of the local government accountants, for whom the statement of changes in equity and the statement of cash flows were also considered as the most dispensable statements (Dasí, Gimeno, & Vela, 2018).

On the other hand, most respondents consider cash surplus statement (included in the notes to financial statements) and the statement of financial position as the documents that are most useful when appraising the financial position.

Regarding this issue, it should be noted that the liquidity and solvency of subnational governments depend on two key aspects, not revealed by the statement of financial position and the statement of financial performance: the ability to establish additional taxes and the likelihood of a rescue by a higher level of government (Anessi-Pessina, Nasi, & Steccolini, 2010). In this sense, it is possible that the financial statements prepared in accordance with the accrual principle have not been adequately designed to reflect the peculiarities of the financial position of the public sector organizations.

One of the most important purposes of governmental accounting is to offer useful and relevant information for those responsible for public management; therefore, in addition to traditional financial and budgetary information, one of the main novelties introduced by the GGAP-2010 is the information on costs of activities and budgetary and economic indicators as a part of notes to the financial statements. In that sense, the interviewees consider the information provided by the budgetary indicators of greater utility, putting the financial and efficiency indicators in a second level. Economic indicators are the ones that are considered less useful.

The governments of the EU elaborate two main types of financial data on their activities, resulting from the existence of two different accounting information systems: Government Financial Statistics (GFS) for fiscal policy purposes, based on the national accounting system (macro system);

and accounting and budgetary reports for accountability and decision-making purposes, relating to individual entities or groups of entities (micro system). In the macro system, GFS reporting guidelines are linked to the System of National Accounts (SNA) and in European System of Accounts-ESA 2010. For the micro systems, International Public Sector Accounting Standards (IPSAS), which address the financial reporting needs of public sector entities around the world, are being used as a basis for a future set of European Public Sector Accounting Standards (EPSAS). The relationship between the different types of reporting is important, in terms of transparency and efficiency, because the micro systems of government accounting systems are generally the data source for compiling GFS (Dasí et al., 2016).

Given the high levels of debt and deficits reached by governments during the deep crisis of recent years, it is considered essential that public entities prepare information that allows to account for the financial situation and the monitoring of stability objectives. At the EU level, one of the objectives with top priority is to control the deficit and the debt of Member States, in order to safeguard the Economic and Monetary Union and guarantee fiscal sustainability (Montesinos, Dasí, & Brusca, 2019). Macroeconomic information, based on the European System of National Accounts, is the one that has served as a basis for controlling the achievement of these objectives. In addition, it is expected that the application of IPSAS will allow the approximation of public sector accounts and national accounts, which would allow more reliable information for the control of fiscal discipline (Jorge, Jesús, & Laureano, 2016).

Currently, EU Member States obtain national accounts through adjustments to the budget accounting, where important differences among countries can be found, both in the number and the amount of these adjustments (Dasí et al., 2013, 2014, 2016; Dasí, Montesinos, & Vela, 2018). As Dabbicco (2018) points out, moving the IPSAS and GFS reporting systems to a common conceptual base is not straightforward, taking into account their different purposes, and that some differences remain because the accounting and statistical communities want it.

In Spain, the three fiscal rules that constitute the three pillars of the public policy to deal with the impact of the economic and financial crisis in public finances are budgetary stability, financial sustainability, and the spending rule. Furthermore, the budgetary stability was considered as a guiding principle for governmental policies, and it was so included when reforming article 135 of Spanish Constitution in 2011.

Therefore, we also included a question about the convenience of incorporate in financial reporting a set of additional information currently not required. This additional information specifically refers to:

a) National Accounting figures
b) Suppliers average terms of payment
c) Economic and financial plans that have been presented and their degree of compliance
d) Reconciliation between budgetary and operative result
e) Rule of Expenditure compliance
f) Transition between the public accounts budget balance and (Budgetary Result) and net lending/borrowing

Data concerning national accounting figures, suppliers' average terms of payment, and compliance with the expenditure rule are considered the most relevant information to be included in regional governmental reporting.

Given that budgetary information constitutes, as stated, the main source for obtaining national accounting figures and compilation of GFS at the international level, we also asked about the convenience of a unification of criteria in budgetary and accrual accounting rules. The 81.25% (13 of 16) of the respondents agree with the criteria unification.

On the other hand, it is necessary to highlight that in public sector there are entities which apply the Business Accounting Plan, but they also must adjust their reports to budgetary regulations. According to Regional Audit Institutions (OCEX, 2017), this hybrid character is the cause of multiple errors, both conceptual and formal, and as a result the budgetary information reported by these public entities is not satisfactory. This fact could be related with the positive responses (93.75%) about the convenience of establishing clear criteria for the conciliation between budget and financial information.

Given the decentralization of public services with the consequent proliferation of public instrumental entities, the questionnaire asked about the usefulness of consolidated financial statements. More than half of the respondents (9 of 16) declare the highest level of usefulness. These results differ from the studies at local level of Dasí, Gimeno, and Vela (2018) and Gomes, Brusca, and Fernandes (2019). As Gomes et al. (2019) point out, in Spain, consolidated statements are not used for management or for decision making because there is not a legal requirement for using them. The professionals who voluntarily prepare consolidated statements said that budgetary reporting was being used for accountability and decision making. The reason may be the large number of instrumental entities that exist at the regional level with respect to the local level.

4.4 Local Government Reform

4.4.1 *The Main Features of Financial Reporting in Spanish Local Governments*

The third level of the decentralized government is the local government, which comprises municipalities, provinces, counties, and the decentralized entities of all the above.

In Spain there are 8131 municipalities, with a great variety between them, in terms of size and economic activities. The largest municipality is Madrid (3,132,463 inhabitants) and the smallest is Illán de Vacas, in Toledo (6 inhabitants). A total of 84% municipalities have less than 5000 inhabitants, but only 13% of the population live in them. Furthermore, there are other 4875 local entities including provinces, counties, and other minor local entities. The number of entities depending on the whole local government is 4563.

The main characteristic of the local government is that it is regulated by central government, differently than the autonomous communities, with more autonomy. There is a common legal framework established by central government for local government financial management, that at the moment is defined in the law 7/1985, regulating the basis of local government and the law 39/1988, regulating local administration (updated subsequently in different occasions). These laws contain the framework for the development of accounting and budgetary criteria.

The Ministry of Economy is responsible for approving the accounting standards applicable to local governments, which are always adapted to the GGAP. Financial accounting based on accrual basis was implemented in 1992 and, since then, local governments have always followed similar principles to the central government. Nevertheless, its adaptation takes always some years and standards are applied with some delays.

After the passing of a new GGAP in 2010, the IGAE started some preparatory works to adapt it to local governments. The new standard was passed in October 2013 and was compulsory for the financial statements of 2015. Therefore, since 2015, the Spanish Local Government is applying accounting standards adapted to IPSAS.

Nevertheless, the budget is prepared according to a modified cash basis and this has not been modified in the accounting reforms. As in the central government, there is a link between the financial accounting system, based on the accrual principle, and the budgetary system, based on modified cash accounting.

Taking into account the local governments size, there are three different models of accounting standards, depending on budget and population. These are the options:

- Basic model, applicable to entities with budgetary revenues lower than 300,000 euros. In this model, it is allowed the use of the cash accounting system and double entry bookkeeping is not necessary. The financial reporting is exclusively budgetary reporting.
- Simplified model, which can be applied to entities that have a budget lower than 3 million euros and fewer than 5000 inhabitants. Double entry bookkeeping is compulsory and financial accounting uses the accrual basis. There are, however, some simplifications for the presentation of financial statements and in some principles for measurement and recognition of assets and liabilities (e.g., in financial assets).
- Normal model, which must be applied to entities that exceed the limits for simplified model. This model is similar to the one applied by central government, and based on the GGAP.

In simplified and normal models, the system produces two types of reports: financial accounting reports (balance sheet, operative statement, cash flow statement, and statement of changes in net assets/equity) and budgetary statements (statement of execution of the budget). The financial statements are adapted to the IPSAS 1 and IPSAS 3, and the standards contain specific rules for their presentation. For example, it can be highlighted that the operative statement contains a classification of expenses by nature instead of a functional classification. The presentation of budgetary reports aims to inform about the different phases of execution of expenditures and revenues. Furthermore, there is no reconciliation between accounting and budgeting reporting in the financial report.

The application of the new system in 2015 led some changes in measurement and recognition of financial statement elements, as well as in the presentation of financial information, in accordance with the IPSAS. The aim of the reform was to adapt the system to the GGAP-2010, which at the same time has had as reference the accounting system of the business entities. Thus, the Anglo-Saxon tradition of attending to economic reality and not only its legal form is imposed.

Therefore, the main differences highlighted for central government could also be pointed out for local government. In this respect, it is important to take into account the diversity of local governments size, because one of the debates that emerged was about the convenience of the new system for the smaller entities (included in the simplified model for example), due to its complexity.

According to Vela, Polo, and Pérez (2016), these are some of the key issues of the reform: (a) the system is complex, due to the influence of business accounting, especially for small entities; (b) the structure of the financial statements is also based on the business sector, which introduces some bias about the relevance of the information. Furthermore, the users do not consider the information related with the financial situation very useful; (c) it would be convenient to prepare some abbreviated information that can be useful also for users with a lack of financial and accounting culture. The last recommendation is in line with the new trend of preparing popular reporting for local governments (Cohen & Karatzimas, 2015).

Accounting standards for local government are adapted to the GGAP and therefore to the IPSAS; however consolidated statements are not compulsory at this level of government. This means that IPSAS 35 about the preparation of consolidated statements is not applied in local government, in spite of different efforts that have tried to implement consolidated reporting in local government (Brusca, Grossi, & Manes Rossi, 2018). The decentralization of local governments for providing services to citizens has been one of the characteristics of governmental reform in the last years, and some governments have a complex group of entities, with some autonomous agencies and business entities depending on the main government. As a consequence, individual statements are considered insufficient to provide information about the financial situation of the group of entities (Vela et al., 2016). In 2015 the IGAE issued a standard for the consolidation of financial statements in the public sector, and the initial aim was to apply it to local government in 2017, but it has been postponed and there are no preparatory works for its implementation. This has been considered by academics one of the deficiencies of the system (Vela et al., 2016), due to the relevance of the dependent entities in some governments, especially in the biggest.

4.4.2 *The Experience of Practitioners*

In order to reveal the experiences of practitioners in municipalities, a survey was designed and carried out for Portuguese and Spanish local governments. The last chapter will present the comparative analysis of the results in order to show the advantages and disadvantages of the reform in both cases and whether the context in which the standards have been implemented affects the success of the standards. In this chapter, some results are presented about the usefulness and use of financial reporting in order to understand what is the opinion of financial managers about the output of the accounting system.

The design and elaboration of the survey have been based on the literature review and documentary analysis of the standards and regulation in both countries. Furthermore, in order to check that the questionnaire was well designed and its understanding by the practitioners, we did a test with a Spanish and a Portuguese financial director.

The questionnaire used a five-point Likert scale and was developed on the web with Google Tools. It was then sent via email to financial directors of the two countries. We asked the financial director to directly answer it or to give it to the accounting officers if they consider this necessary or convenient.

In Spain, the questionnaire was sent to 400 Spanish municipalities, randomly selected from three groups according with the size (fewer than 20,000 inhabitants, between 20,000 and 100,000 and higher than 100,000 inhabitants), in order to have a similar number of municipalities to the Portuguese sample. Data collection was carried out between April 2018 and March 2019. From 400 questionnaires, 197 have been returned (response rate of 49.25%), distributed as follows: 121 (61%) from entities with less than 20,000 inhabitants, 61 (31%) from entities between 20,000 and 100,000 inhabitants, and 15 (8%) from entities higher than 100,000 inhabitants.

a) The usefulness of financial reporting and performance indicators

In order to know the opinion of practitioners about the accounting system, one of the questions of the survey referred to the usefulness of the financial statements. The statement that has higher valuation is the budget execution statement (mean of 4.69 over 5), that is prepared with the modified cash accounting criteria. In total, 95% of the respondents consider this information very useful (punctuation of 4 or 5).

On the opposite side, the statement of changes in net assets and the cash flow statement (mean of 2.33 and 2.60 over five, respectively), introduced by the new standards as a consequence of the adaptation to the IPSAS, are considered of low usefulness. This indicates that financial directors do not see added value in the new financial statements taken into account by the IPSAS. Also the statement of financial position and the statement of financial performance are considered with low usefulness by a high percentage of the financial directors (only 31% give values of 4 or 5, the mean being 2.63 and 2.72 respectively).

This means that budgetary reporting continues being more useful than accrual financial statements, which may be due to characteristics of the legal and administrative system, as political decisions and deliberations are based on the budget. The Council approves the budget and the political control is based on the budget execution and even the legal control is based on the execution of the budget. This gives to the budget a preponderance with respect to accrual financial statements.

This is in line with the results of previous literature in other countries and contexts (Cohen et al., 2019; van Helden, 2016), the needs of accounting information depend on the administrative system in place, and some mismatches can emerge. When the laws do not require the use of accrual accounting for decision making and accountability purposes, then the usefulness of accrual accounting will be reduced.

The accounting standards require that financial reports include five kinds of indicators: budgetary, financial, economy, efficiency, and efficacy indicators. The results show again that budgetary indicators are considered the most useful (mean of 3.70 out of 5). After that, the economy indicators (mean of 3.38 out 5) and the financial indicators (3.09 out of 5) are placed. The efficiency and efficacy indicators are not considered very useful (mean of 2.82 and 2.85 respectively), which can be due to the difficulties to obtain this information and the lack of standardization of the indicators. In fact, in most of the entities the indicators are not included in the reports.

b) The use of financial reporting

The questionnaire contained a specific question about the use of the information for different purposes. The results show that the information is used mainly for accountability purposes, but also for elaborating the budget of future years, which explains again the usefulness of budgetary reporting. Financial directors give a high assessment to the use of information for accountability purposes (mean of 3.52 out of 5). The law requires local governments to submit the financial report to the Supreme Audit Institution and to a Regional Audit Institution, as well as to publish the report on the web. This can explain that directors consider that the main purpose of the financial report is accountability to stakeholders.

A high percentage of respondents consider also that the information is used for the elaboration of the budget of the following year (mean of 3.16 out of 5), and 47% of the respondents give values of 4 or 5. In Spain, local governments prepare program budgeting with a classification of expenditures by nature, and traditional budgeting is maintained. Although standards are focused on programs and objectives, in practice incremental budgeting is used in many cases, which can explain the relevance of budgetary data for preparing the budget of the next year.

With the exception of budgetary management, the results evidence that the use of information for management purposes is very low. For example, only 25% said that the information is used for management decisions (mean of 2.39 out of 5), and 22% consider important the use for planning and management control (mean of 2.52% out of 5).

c) Consolidated financial statements

In Spain, for local governments consolidated reporting is not compulsory in accrual financial statements, but optional, and the municipal council can decide about its elaboration. Nevertheless, for the budget, consolidated reporting is compulsory. The reporting entity in the case of the budget includes the municipality, the autonomous agencies created, and municipal enterprises in which the municipality has the 100% of equity. This criterion does not coincide with the concept of control used by IPSAS for the elaboration of consolidated financial statements.

In the analysis of the responses to the questionnaire, 57 entities out of the 197 confirm that they prepare consolidated reporting, but in most of the cases it is just the consolidated budget and consolidated statement of budget execution. Only 18 entities prepare a consolidated balance sheet, corresponding to the biggest entities.

A high percentage of practitioners (52.8%) consider that it would be useful to prepare accrual consolidated financial statements, but there are still many of them that do not see value added in preparing consolidated reporting using accrual criteria, which once again shows that in many local governments accrual has not been embedded in public sector financial management.

We have included also a question asking about the uses of consolidated financial statements and the financial directors consider that it will be useful to inform about the financial situation and budgetary execution of all the entities of the group, but mainly for accountability purposes. They do not consider that this can help in management and making decisions about how to provide public services.

4.5 Critical Analysis of the Advantages and Disadvantages of IPSAS Implementation

The governmental accounting standards in Spain are contained in the GGAP, which establish the general framework for public administration and it is based on business accounting standards and IPSAS. The GGAP was approved in 2010 but it is not directly applicable to the administrations. For each level of government there is an adaptation of the GGAP. The decentralized structure of the Spanish public sector is the reason for the existence of particular regulations for the central, regional, and local governments. The central government, and in particular the IGAE, issues the standards for central and local governments, while the regional governments establish their own accounting regulations, which are normally adapted to the central framework.

Accounting standards adapted to the GGAP have been applied in central government since 2011 and in local government since 2015, while in the regional governments the situation is diverse because of the different adaptation schedules. The FLA of 2014 has been an important driver for updating the regional adaptations to the GGAP, reducing differences in regional regulations.

The opinion of the preparers of the information about the convenience of the new system and the usefulness of the information prepared is also very different in the three levels of governments, possibly due to the differences in the context of the three levels. Nevertheless, a common characteristic is that budgetary reporting is still considered more useful than accrual financial statements.

In the central government, the preparers consider that the application of the new system is adequate and fits the Spanish context well. One of the main advantages of the new system has been the homogenization of criteria for different entities across the public sector (administrative organisms, business and nonprofit entities, such as foundations), improving the quality of financial reporting and making the elaboration of consolidated statements easier. Central government prepares consolidated financial reporting in accordance with IPSAS and all the dependent entities are included in the financial statements. The information is mainly used for accountability purposes, both to citizens and to the Supreme Audit Institution, while for decision making, strategic decision about public policies, management control, and performance measurement, its use is low. The preparers still value budgetary reporting more than accrual financial reporting. The cash flow statement is also very useful, but the income statement and the statement of changes in the net asset are not very appreciated.

The auditors also consider that the new system has improved the quality of financial reporting and that the elaboration of consolidated statements has been an important advance. They also recognize that in Spain, the use of the information is higher for accountability purposes than for decision making.

Both preparers and auditors recognize the advantages of the new system because of the improvements in the quality of reporting and the homogenization of criteria with business entities. However, there are also some difficulties related to the training of human resources and the involvement of politicians and senior management.

In regional governments, accounting managers believe that the new regulatory framework is better suited to the context of regional administrations than the previous one; they also think that it makes the consolidation of the financial statements easier, improves accountability, and introduces more appropriate measurement criteria.

Among the disadvantages and difficulties of the new model the regional governments accountants highlight the lack of means and technical support, as well as the lack of participation and political interest and the excessive bureaucracy in the public administration as the most significant factors to explain the delay observed in the adaptation to the GGAP framework and rules at regional level.

The respondents from regional governments rate budgetary reporting highly and consider that the statement of financial position is useful when evaluating the financial position of public entities. However, they consider the statement of changes in net assets/equity and the cash flow statement less useful and that they could be eliminated from the annual financial statements. Regarding the indicators to be included in the financial reports, the interviewees consider the budgetary indicators as the most useful, followed by the financial ones and those of efficiency, while the economic indicators are the least useful. Furthermore, given the existence of various types of dependent public entities, such as commercial companies, foundations, consortiums, and agencies, it is considered necessary to prepare consolidated financial statements, to provide a global vision of the activity carried out by each public group and will facilitate the comparability of accounting reporting between entities, especially as regards the temporary evolution of their financial situation.

In the local governments, financial directors consider that accrual financial statements have limited usefulness and value budgetary reporting more highly. One of the main reasons is that the laws refer to the use of budgetary information for different purposes, such as the control of budgetary stability, while the use of accrual reporting is not required for management or decision-making purposes. Therefore, the financial directors consider that the information is mainly used for accountability purposes and the audit institutions (central and regional) are considered the main users of the information. Consolidation of financial statements is voluntary for accrual accounting and a high percentage of respondents consider consolidated reporting useful, but there are still many financial directors that do not consider that this has an important value added in the local government context. One of the difficulties is that the financial directors consider accrual financial reporting a complex system, which makes it necessary to invest in training and technologies. Furthermore, and in spite of the requirement to publish financial statements on the web, citizens are not considered important users of this information because it is difficult to understand. One important conclusion is that information should be presented as simply as possible and probably requires to prepare some abbreviated and synthetic reporting to citizens, in the line proposed by popular reporting.

References

Anessi-Pessina, E., Nasi, G., & Steccolini, I. (2010). Accounting innovations: A contingent view on Italian local governments. *Journal of Public Budgeting, Accounting & Financial Management, 22*(2), 250–271.

Ballart, X., & Zapico, E. (2010). Budget reforms in Spain. In J. Wanna, L. Jensen, & J. de Vries (Eds.), *The reality of budget reform: Counting the consequences in 11 advanced democracies* (p. 2010). London: Elgar.

Brusca, I., Grossi, G., & Manes-Rossi, F. (2018). Setting consolidated reporting standards for local government. *Public Money & Management, 38*(7), 483–492.
Brusca, I., & Montesinos, V. (2013). From rhetoric to practice: The case of Spanish local government reforms. *Financial Accountability and Management, 29*(4), 354–377.
Cohen, S., & Karatzimas, S. (2015). Tracing the future of reporting in the public sector: Introducing integrated popular reporting. *International Journal of Public Sector Management, 28*(6), 449–460.
Cohen, S., Manes Rossi, F., Caperchione, E., & Brusca, I. (2019). Local government administration systems and local government accounting information needs: Is there a mismatch? *International Review of Administrative Science, 85*(4), 708–725.
Dabbicco, G. (2018). A comparison of debt measures in fiscal statistics and public sector financial statements. *Public Money & Management, 38*(7), 511–518.
Dasí, R., Montesinos, V., & Murgui, S. (2016). Government financial statistics and accounting in Europe: Is ESA 2010 improving convergence? *Public Money and Management, 36*(3), 165–172.
Dasí, R., Montesinos, V., & Vela, J. M. (2018). Towards convergence of government financial statistics and accounting in Europe at central and local levels. *Revista de Contabilidad-Spanish Accounting Review, 21*(2), 140–149.
Dasí, R. M., Gimeno, A., & Vela, J. M. (2018). The recent reform of Spanish local governmental accounting: A critical perspective from local governmental accountants as internal users of budgeting and financial accounting information. *Lex Localis – Journal of Local Self-Government, 16*(3), 453–473.
Dasí, R. M., Montesinos, V., & Murgui, S. (2013). Comparative analysis of governmental accounting diversity in the European Union. *Journal of Comparative Policy Analysis: Research and Practice, 15*(3), 255–273.
Dasí, R. M., Montesinos, V., & Murgui, S. (2014). La convergencia de los sistemas de contabilidad pública en Europa como escenario para el nuevo Sistema de Cuentas Nacionales. *Spanish Journal of Finance and Accounting, 43*(4), 424–448.
European Commission. (2013). *Report from the commission to the council and the European Parliament, towards implementing harmonized public sector accounting standards in member states.* Brussels, Belgium: European Commission.
GASB. (1987). *Concepts statement n° 1 objectives of financial reporting.* Norwalk, CT: GASB.
Gomes, P., Brusca, I., & Fernandes, M. J. (2019). Implementing the international public sector accounting standards for consolidated financial statements: Facilitators, benefits and challenges. *Public Money & Management, 39*(8), 544–552.
IFAC (International Federation of Accountants). (2012). *Reporting on the long-term sustainability of a public sector entity's finances.* New York: IFAC.

IFAC (International Federation of Accountants). (2014). *Public sector conceptual framework*. New York: IFAC.
IMF. (2017). *Fiscal Affairs Department (FAD): How to select fiscal rules; A primer*. Retrieved from https://www.imf.org
IPSASB. (2018). *Handbook of international public sector accounting standards*. New York: IPSASB.
Jorge, S., Jesus, M., & Laureano, R. (2016). Governmental accounting maturity toward IPSASs and the approximation to national accounts in the European Union. *International Journal of Public Administration, 39*(12), 976–988.
Montesinos, V., Dasí, R., & Brusca, I. (2019). A framework for comparing financial sustainability in EU countries: National accounts, governmental accounting and the challenge of harmonization. In J. Caruana, I. Brusca, E. Caperchione, S. Cohen, & F. M. Rossi (Eds.), *Financial sustainability of public sector entities: The relevance of accounting frameworks* (pp. 41–61). Palgrave Macmillan.
Montesinos, V., Pina, V., Torres, L., & Vela, J. M. (1998). Análisis comparado de los principios y prácticas contables de los sistemas contables públicos de los países de la OCDE: una aproximación empírica. *Spanish Journal of Finance and Accounting, 96*, 787–820.
Montesinos, V., Vela, J. M., & Benito, B. (2001). Accounting and financial reporting in Spanish regional governments: Exploring similarities and differences. In A. Bac (Ed.), *International comparative issues in government accounting* (pp. 195–212). New York: Springer US.
OCEX (ÓRGANOS AUTONÓMICOS DE CONTROL EXTERNO) (2017). *Conclusiones de los XII Encuentros Técnicos y VII Foro Tecnológico Barcelona*, 28 y 29 de septiembre de 2017. BOLETÍN NOVIEMBRE 2017. https://asocex.es/wp-content/uploads/2017/11/OCEX-BOLETIN-n%C2%BA-17.pdf
Pollitt, C., & Bouckaert, G. (2017). *Public management reform: A comparative analysis-into the age of austerity*. Oxford, UK: Oxford University Press.
PwC (Price Waterhouse Coopers). (2017, November). *Member States' approaches to harmonising charts of accounts for national purposes with a view to financial reporting requirements under the future European public sector accounting standards*. EPSAS. Retrieved from https://circabc.europa.eu
van Helden, J. (2016). Literature review and challenging research agenda on politicians' use of accounting information. *Public Money & Management, 36*(7), 531–538.
van Helden, J., & Reichard, C. (2018). Cash or accruals for budgeting? Why some governments in Europe changed their budgeting mode and others not. *OECD Journal on Budgeting, 18*(1), 91–113.
Vela, J. M., Polo, F., & Pérez, S. (2016). La reforma de la Contabilidad de la Administración Local española: algunas reflexiones críticas en torno a las nuevas instrucciones de contabilidad. *Ciriec ESPAÑA, Revista de Economía Pública, Social y Cooperativa, 86*, 221–250.

CHAPTER 5

Comparative Analysis Between Portugal and Spain

Patrícia Gomes, Isabel Brusca, Maria José Fernandes, and Vicente Montesinos

Abstract This chapter comparatively analyzes Portugal and Spain in relation to the implementation of the IPSAS-based accounting system as two European continental countries embedded in the Napoleonic administrative tradition and considered "latecomers" in the NPM reforms. It adds

P. Gomes (✉) • M. J. Fernandes
Department of Accounting and Taxation, Polytechnic Institute of Cávado and Ave, Barcelos, Portugal
e-mail: pgomes@ipca.pt; mjfernandes@ipca.pt

I. Brusca
Department of Accounting and Finance, University of Zaragoza, Zaragoza, Spain
e-mail: ibrusca@unizar.es

V. Montesinos
Department of Accounting, University of Valencia, Valencia, Spain
e-mail: Vicente.Montesinos@uv.es

I. Brusca et al. (eds.), *Challenges in the Adoption of International Public Sector Accounting Standards*, Public Sector Financial Management, https://doi.org/10.1007/978-3-030-63125-3_5

knowledge about the differences in the harmonization process and in the operationalization of the new accounting system in these particular contexts. Main findings show that IPSAS and the IFRS-based business accounting system have been important references for the new public sector accounting system in both countries. On the other hand, although Spain is more experienced in operationalizing the new IPSAS-based accounting system, we find that the country adopts a more sceptical approach of the boundaries of the new standards than Portugal.

Keywords IPSAS • Portugal • Spain • Comparative analysis

5.1 A Comparison of the Normative Process: Drivers and Actors

Like Southern European countries, Portugal and Spain are characterized by their traditional bureaucracies, centralized hierarchical organizational structures and centralized decision-making. Nevertheless, the governments of both countries have implemented, by law, several administrative reforms in the last two decades (Brusca, Montesinos, & Chow, 2013; Gomes, Fernandes, & Carvalho, 2015) as part of a broader set of NPM initiatives. They are considered "latecomers" in the implementation of NPM reforms, but both have more than 20 years of experience in accrual accounting and accounting reforms.

In Spain, accrual accounting was introduced in the public sector in the 1980s, and local governments have been using accrual financial statements since 1992. Business accounting principles and methodology have always been important references for the public sector (Jorge, Brusca, & Nogueira, 2019).

Because of this, reforms in business accounting standards due to the European Union strategy of applying International Accounting Standards (IAS) and IFRS also had some implications for the public sector. In 2007, the accounting standards for the business sector were adapted by the IFRS, starting a process of reform that led to a new accounting plan for the public sector in 2010. The accounting plan was prepared considering two references: accounting standards for the business sector and the international standards of the IPSASB (both based on IFRS). Consequently, the accounting plan passed in 2010 incorporates most of the accounting principles contained in IPSAS at that moment, recognizing that the standards have gained legitimacy at the international level. For the local government, the new accounting standard, adapted to IPSAS, was approved in 2013 and has been applied since 2015. Thus, accounting standards and financial statements preparation are patterned after international standards, and recognition and measurement principles resemble those of the international standards. However, the accounting plan does not refer to consolidated accounts because they are not compulsory for the local government. Furthermore, the modified cash budget is maintained, with an integrated system between financial statements and budgetary reporting.

In Portugal, an important driver in the decision to adapt public accounting to IPSAS was the approval of the new IFRS-based business accounting system (SNC) in July 2009, becoming effective on January 1, 2010. As public sector accounting has followed business sector regulation, the new regulation led to a debate about the reform in the public sector. The reform in business sector accounting led to a difference in the standards of public and private sectors that hampered the process of consolidation (Gomes, Brusca, & Fernandes, 2019). These problems led to the approval of Order 474/2010 for the public sector, aiming at the standardization and homogenization of the consolidation process. The preamble stated that the standard for the consolidation of accounts for the public sector should be based on IPSAS. Thus, this was really the first step toward adopting IPSAS. Nevertheless, other factors have stimulated public sector accounting reforms: the financial crisis and lender pressures (e.g., from the IMF). At the same time, there was an internal demand from professionals of a more complete accounting system, as some operations were not regulated, such as public–private partnerships (Gomes et al., 2015; Jorge et al., 2019).

As a consequence of these pressures, the Portuguese government created the CNCP, which elaborated the new public sector accounting system based on IPSAS—the SNC-AP. The implementation process began in January 2018 (although it permits the possibility of municipalities delaying the initiation until 2020). The actual SNC-AP, simultaneously adopting IPSAS and endorsing internal and international harmonization, included several adaptations to the Portuguese reality, such as restricting some options allowed by IPSAS and creating three particular standards on budgetary accounting and reporting (NCP 26), management accounting (NCP 27), and a simplified financial accounting regime for smaller entities (NCP-PE).

There are many similarities between Portugal and Spain in their public sector accounting tradition, where accounting standards assume a legal form, making changes more difficult, and where professional influence in accounting policymaking is low. However, Jorge et al. (2019) found that public sector accounting standard setters have been an important actor in the process of IPSAS enrolment by both Iberian countries. The studies of Gomes et al. (2015) and Brusca et al. (2013) reinforce these results for Portugal and Spain, respectively. Therefore, prior studies reveal that different drivers influence the decision to implement the IPSAS-based accounting system in the public sectors of the two countries.

Comparing the normative in both countries, Table 5.1 presents a synthesis of the main stages of reforms carried out in the last two decades. Some important highlights are as follows:

- The reform in Spain has always been an important reference for those implemented in Portugal because legal requirements have been first approved by the Spanish government and followed (with adaptations and some changes) by the Portuguese government.
- Spain has a general accounting plan, and different adaptations are approved for the three levels of government (central, regional, and local), as well as for health entities. Similarly, in Portugal, a general accounting plan has been approved for the central government, and adaptations are introduced for the local government and for specific sectors such as education, health, and social security.
- The adaptation of the business accounting system to IFRS has been an important driver for an accounting system adapted to IPSAS in the public sector.
- IPSAS and the business accounting system based on IFRS have been important references for the new public sector accounting system in both countries.
- Standard setters have been important actors of the reform; in Portugal, the financial crisis and lender pressures also played an important role in the decision to adopt IPSAS.
- The new IPSAS-based accounting system in Spain includes two accounting systems (budgeting and financial) although the SNC-AP in Portugal includes three (budgeting, financial, and management); this reflects different views in preparing and presenting management accounting indicators that will help decision-making.

Table 5.1 Comparison of the normative process in the Iberian Peninsula

Spain		*Portugal*	
1977	General Budgetary law (it marks the beginning of the reform)	**1990**	Public Sector Accounting Basis Law
1983	First General Governmental Accounting Plan (GGAP)	**1991**	New Budget Framework Law
1990	First Adaptation of GGAP to the local government. First financial statements prepared with accrual in local government in 1992	**1992**	Regulatory law of the State Financial Management (1992)
1994	Reform of the GGAP to adapt it to the business sector accounting plan of 1990	**1997**	First Chart of Accounts for Public Sector (POCP)
2004–2006	Adaptation of local government accounting to the reformed GGAP, applied since 2006.	**1999**	First Chart of Accounts for Local Government (POCAL)
2007	Business sector accounting adapted to IFRSs—new Business Accounting Plan (starting implementation in 2008)	**2000**	First Chart of Accounts for the Education Sector First Chart of Accounts for the Health Sector
2010	Reform of the GGAP to adapt it to the Business Accounting Plan and the IPSAS	**2002**	First Chart of Accounts for the Entities of the Social Security System (POCISSS)
2013–2015	Reform of the adaptation to the GGAP for local government, adapting it to 2010 GGAP. Compulsory since 2015	**2009**	Business sector accounting adapted to IFRSs—SNC, starting implementation in 2010

(*continued*)

Table 5.1 (continued)

Spain		*Portugal*	
2016–2019	Adaptation of several regional governments to the 2010 GGAP	**2013–2015**	Reform of the public sector Chart of Accounts to adapt it to the IPSAS and the new business Chart of Accounts (starting implementation in 2018) New Budget Framework Law (2015) System of Accounting Standards for Public Administrations (SNC-AP)—embracing a simplified regime for small public sector entities
		2016	Approval of the simplified regime for small and micro public sector entities (SME) Creation of UniLEO, the unit responsible for the implementation and diffusion of the SNC-AP, under the Ministry of Finance
		2018	First year of reporting according SNC-AP (for central government)
		2019	Order n° 1/2019 of the Court of Auditors—clarifies the reporting process to the Court of Auditors and obligates to its electronic submission through a centralized electronic platform developed in articulation by the Ministry of Finance and the UniLEO

– The presentation of consolidated financial statements for local governments has been compulsory in Portugal since 2010, but in Spain, this is only a voluntary practice despite different efforts to introduce consolidated reporting in local government (Gomes et al., 2019).

- Both countries have three different reporting regimes with varying applicability. In Portugal, there is a normal regime (for entities with budgets higher than five million euros), a regime for small entities (for entities with a budget higher than one million euros but less than five million euros), and a regime for micro entities (with budgets lower than one million euros); in Spain, the normal regime is applicable for budgets higher than three million euros or more than 5000 inhabitants, the simplified regime for entities with budgets lower than three million, and the basic model for entities with budgetary revenues lower than 300,000 euros.

5.2 Comparing the Advantages and Disadvantages of IPSAS Implementation

5.2.1 Research Design

The aim of this section is to take stock of the experiences of Spain and Portugal in the adoption of IPSAS, focusing on the advantages and difficulties of the process. To reveal the experiences of practitioners in municipalities, the research design is based on a survey addressed/applied to Portuguese and Spanish local governments. The section adopts a comparative analysis of the results to determine whether the context in which the standards have been implemented affects the success of the standards. An original questionnaire has been created, which considers the literature review and feedback obtained from interviews with the financial directors of some municipalities in Spain and Portugal. These interviews represent a pilot test in the construction and validation of the questionnaire. The Google Drive platform was used for the questionnaire, using a five-point Likert scale. The survey questions reflect the perception of respondents relating the new IPSAS-based accounting system, including appropriateness (Q1), advantages (Q2), difficulties (Q3), and measures for success (Q4).

We have chosen the local governments of both countries for comparison because the local context seems to be the subsector where the accrual-based accounting system is implemented to a greater extent (Brusca, Caperchione, Cohen, & Manes-Rossi, 2015; Gomes et al., 2015; Pina, Torres, & Yetano, 2009; PwC, 2014).

Table 5.2 Size of the local governments that have responded

Position held	*Total*		*%*	
	Spain	*Portugal*	*Spain*	*Portugal*
Fewer than 20,000 inhabitants	121	67	61%	54%
Between 20,000 and 100,000 inhabitants	61	43	31%	34%
Higher than 100,000 inhabitants	15	15	8%	12%
Total	197	125	100%	100%

In Portugal, the questionnaire was sent to 308 municipalities, and data collection was carried out between March and December 2018. Of 308 questionnaires, 125 were returned (response rate of 41%). The questionnaire was also sent to 400 Spanish municipalities, randomly selected from three groups according to size (below 20,000 inhabitants, between 20,000 and 100,000, and above 100,000 inhabitants) to have a similar number of municipalities. Data collection was carried out between April 2018 and March 2019. Of 400 questionnaires, 197 were returned (response rate of 49.25%).

The distribution of respondents according to size is shown in Table 5.2. The higher percentage of responses is from entities below 20,000 inhabitants (61% and 54% for Spain and Portugal, respectively); on average, only 10% of the sample is composed of municipalities with more than 100,000 inhabitants (8% for Spain and 12% for Portugal).

Considering the profile of the respondents, the sample is mainly composed of financial directors, accounting chiefs, and accounting technicians.

The use of these two subsamples (Portugal and Spain) aims to compare the two countries' perception of the reform of local government accounting in two different contexts; Portugal is in the transition process of implementing the new accounting system, and Spain has already been applying IPSAS since 2015 for local governments. Data are analyzed using descriptive statistics and comparative analysis between the two subsamples to check the differences between the two countries, which will be explained in the next section.

5.2.2 *Analysis of Results*

The respondents' perceptions of the features and the role of the new IPSAS-based accounting system are based on a question about their opinions on the appropriateness of the new accounting system (Q1).

As can be seen in Table 5.3, the Spanish respondents were sceptic about the appropriateness of the new accounting system, as most of the items have values around 3 (out of 5), and the percentage of respondents with high values (4–5) is always less than 50%. However, the Portuguese respondents highly value the adequacy of the new accounting system. In fact, the only item with a higher value in Spain is the following: the new regulation added complexity to the system, but the information is not of greater utility. Of the Spanish respondents, 43% highly agree with this item (levels 4 and 5). The percentage in Portugal is lower for this item (35%). This shows that the professionals in Spanish local governments are not satisfied with the new system. Only 30% of the respondents consider that the new accounting system is more adequate to local government characteristics, decreasing the number of people who consider that the

Table 5.3 Appropriateness of the new accounting system

	Spain				*Portugal*			
	Mean	*SD*	*Min/ Max*	*4–5*	*Mean*	*SD*	*Min/ Max*	*4–5*
I believe that the new information system is more appropriate	3.16	1.06	1/5	38%	3.70	0.94	1/5	65%
This new accounting system is better suited for local governments	2.95	1.09	1/5	30%	3.45	0.95	1/5	51%
The measurement criteria of the new system are more adequate than the old	2.96	1.07	1/5	30%	3.54	0.91	1/5	55%
The application of fair value seems appropriate	2.88	1.13	1/5	30%	3.42	0.92	1/5	49%
The change adds complexity to the system, but the information is not of greater utility	3.23	1.26	1/5	43%	3.05	1.03	1/5	35%
The new system facilitates the consolidation of accounts	3.11	1.23	1/5	40%	4.01	0.90	1/5	71%
The changes seem to be of little relevance to the context of municipalities	2.78	1.09	1/5	21%	2.80	1.05	1/5	25%

(1—totally disagree; 5—totally agree)

measurement criteria of the new system are more adequate. These percentages are higher for Portugal, where 51% of the respondents consider that the new system fits local government characteristics better (levels 4 and 5). The most important role of the new system is to facilitate the consolidation process in the context of Portugal (71% agree with this).

Concerning the IPSAS implementation process in the Iberian Peninsula, the goal is to understand the respondents' perception concerning three questions: Q2 (the advantages/benefits to adopt the new IPSAS-based accounting system), Q3 (difficulties/obstacles to adopt the new accounting system), and Q4 (measures to ensure the success of the new accounting system).

In the second question, we intend to analyze the main attributes that the literature argues for the new accounting system: quality of information, transparency, accountability, control, standardization, consolidation of accounts, reliability, use of information, and comparability. In Table 5.4, it can be seen again that Portuguese local governments respondents value

Table 5.4 Advantages/benefits of adopting the new accounting system

	Spain				*Portugal*			
	Mean	*SD*	*Min/ Max*	*4–5*	*Mean*	*SD*	*Min/ Max*	*4–5*
Improving the information quality	2.93	1.19	1/5	34%	3.70	0.77	1/5	65%
More transparency of public accounts	2.94	1.22	1/5	35%	3.67	0.88	1/5	61%
More accountability and responsibility	3.14	1.30	1/5	46%	3.70	0.84	1/5	63%
Better control of government actions	2.67	1.20	1/5	26%	3.31	0.88	1/5	40%
Standardization in the disclosure of information	2.94	1.24	1/5	36%	4.06	0.79	1/5	80%
Improve consolidation process	3.01	1.17	1/5	35%	3.93	0.82	1/5	71%
Improving the reliability of public accounts	2.98	1.21	1/5	36%	3.66	0.89	1/5	60%
Use of information for internal decision-making	2.58	1.20	1/5	24%	3.42	0.81	1/5	44%
Use of information for internal control and planning	2.76	1.22	1/5	29%	3.42	0.86	1/5	44%
Increased level of comparability of information	3.03	1.22	1/5	39%	3.98	0.83	1/5	77%

(1—not at all; 5—very great extent)

the potential benefits of the new system more: 65% consider that the new system improves the quality of information (levels 4 and 5), while in Spain, this percentage is just 34%. The standardization in the disclosure of information is the most valuable benefit to Portuguese professionals (80%) followed by the increase in comparability of information (77%), for levels 4 and 5. In Spain, with a lower value, the promotion of accountability and responsibility is the most valuable benefit (46%).

The following question is about the difficulties and obstacles to adopt the new accounting system. As can be seen in Table 5.5, in Spain the main obstacles are the lack of political involvement (69%) followed by the lack of training in the area and the lack of culture in financial matters (63% for levels 4 and 5). These are also important difficulties in the case of Portugal, with the lack of human resources, political and top managers' involvement, and technical support being the obstacles with higher values.

Table 5.5 Difficulties/obstacles of adopting the new accounting system

	Spain				*Portugal*			
	Mean	*SD*	*Min/ Max*	*4–5*	*Mean*	*SD*	*Min/ Max*	*4–5*
Reduced knowledge of the new system	3.28	1.11	1/5	44%	3.50	0.92	1/5	48%
Lack of human resources training in the area	3.73	1.15	1/5	63%	3.71	0.87	2/5	62%
Lack of technical support	3.49	1.23	1/5	50%	3.62	0.95	1/5	56%
Lack of an appropriate information system	3.40	1.21	1/5	46%	3.58	0.96	1/5	54%
Lack of involvement of top management	3.48	1.32	1/5	53%	3.62	0.99	1/5	57%
Lack of political involvement	3.84	1.31	1/5	69%	3.70	1.02	1/5	62%
Reduced utility and little relevance attributed to the information obtained	3.13	1.15	1/5	33%	3.35	0.93	1/5	42%
Resistance to change	3.21	1.19	1/5	40%	3.32	1.08	1/5	46%
Lack of culture in financial matters	3.67	1.19	1/5	63%	3.41	0.99	1/5	48%
Excessive bureaucracy of the public administration	3.79	1.16	1/5	62%	3.57	1.01	1/5	53%

(1—not at all; 5—very great extent)

Our last question aims to analyze what can be done to improve the success of public sector accounting reform. The actions most important for both countries can be highlighted: investment in training and human resources, equipping entities with appropriate information systems, and engagement of managers and politicians. In both countries, these measures have high mean values. The main difference is the need for an independent auditor and to implement internal and external monitoring systems, which are not so important in the Spanish context. This result for Portugal is coherent with conclusions obtained by Jorge et al. (2019) for pilot entities that have experienced SNC-AP earlier. They also consider monitoring an important measure to ensure the success of the reform. Table 5.6 presents descriptive statistics.

Therefore, the results show that *difficulties/obstacles* to adopt the new accounting system are similar for both countries. Thus, they agree in

Table 5.6 Measures to ensure the success of the new accounting system

	Spain				*Portugal*			
	Mean	*SD*	*Min/ Max*	*4–5*	*Mean*	*SD*	*Min/ Max*	*4–5*
Investment in the adequate training of human resources	4.44	0.80	1/5	88%	4.64	0.56	3/5	96%
Equipping entities with appropriate information systems	4.52	0.74	1/5	89%	4.54	0.61	3/5	94%
Obligation to have a certified accountant in public entities (in the preparation of accounts)	4.19	1.02	1/5	79%	3.83	1.00	1/5	62%
Engage top management in the reform process	4.06	1.04	1/5	74%	4.42	0.64	3/5	92%
Obtain political commitment to the implementation of reform	4.21	0.98	1/5	78%	4.38	0.63	3/5	92%
Develop enforcement mechanisms	4.18	0.87	1/5	80%	4.29	0.74	1/5	89%
Require legal certification of accounts by an independent auditor	2.95	1.38	1/5	36%	4.17	0.81	1/5	78%
Ensure internal and external monitoring of system implementation (Court of Auditors, inspections, etc.)	3.36	1.24	1/5	48%	4.05	0.80	1/5	75%

(1—not important; 5—very important)

considering the context of difficulties in which this reform happens. This can be an important contribution for other countries moving toward IPSAS-based accounting standards.

5.3 The Operationalization of Accounting Harmonization in the Public Sector

Portugal and Spain have recently adapted their accounting standards to IPSAS. In Spain, the new IPSAS-like standards have been in effect since 2015 while in Portugal, the initial aim was to apply the new system for 2018, but governments postponed it to 2020 for local offices. In any case, they know the system well, as they were prepared to apply it in 2018. One important factor for the reform in both countries has been the adaptation of business accounting standards to IFRS.

The introduction of accrual financial reporting has been an objective of governments around the world (Hyndman & Connolly, 2011; Lapsley, Mussari, & Paulsson, 2009), mainly generalized after the diffusion of NPM principles (Hood, 1995). In most countries, the reforms have been inspired by private sector management concepts, and tools have been imported into the public sector, considering that this would be a solution for improving management and accountability in the public sector.

In recent years, IPSAS have become an international reference to introduce accrual reporting in many countries. The reform processes have been promoted by various international organizations such as the World Bank or the International Monetary Fund (Adhikari & Mellemvik, 2010; Argento, Peda, & Grossi, 2018; IMF, 2012). Also, the European Commission is leading a process aiming to harmonize public sector accounting in the European Union (European Commission, 2013; Manes Rossi, Cohen, Caperchione, & Brusca, 2016), and IPSAS will be considered as a reference in the development of the European Public Sector Accounting Standards (EPSAS).

The fact is that IPSAS have gained legitimacy, and the literature confirms its endorsement in many countries (Argento et al., 2018; Brusca & Martínez, 2016; Christiaens, Vanhee, Manes-Rossi, Aversano, & Van Cauwenberge, 2015; Jorge et al., 2019), including Portugal and Spain. Both countries have long traditions of preparing accrual financial statements, and the recent reforms have adapted national standards to IPSAS. The main reason has been the reform of private sector accounting to adapt it to the IFRS. In the case of Portugal, the intervention of the Troika during the financial crisis in the period of 2011–2015 was also fundamental in implementing IPSAS (as explained in Chap. 3).

The literature refers to potential benefits to IPSAS adoption, such as increasing accountability and transparency, comparability among governments, or the legitimacy of the standards of governments that implement them. IPSAS, however, have some critics, arguing for example that the spirit and financial logic of IFRS prevails in IPSAS, incorporating short-term logic and financial performance (Ellwood & Newberry, 2007; Hopper, Lassoud, & Soobaroyen, 2017; Oulasvirta, 2014). Following this critical perspective, the EUROSTAT report (2012) stated that, in the opinion of the Portuguese Court of Auditors and the Ministry of Finance, IPSAS do not provide sufficient guidance on the following topics: (1) recognition of the historical heritage (monuments and work of art); (2) liabilities related to social funds (not addressed by IPSAS); (3) tax revenue (no recommendation from IPSAS on the recording of the tax revenue in an accrual basis); and (4) consolidation process (no guidance provided on the definition of controlling and controlled entities from a government perspective). These critics would undermine the reform process, which currently has some technical and managerial problems that remain unsolved (Jorge et al., 2019).

The analysis carried out for Portugal and Spain shows differences in the opinion of professionals of local governments in both countries about the appropriateness of the reform. In Spain, financial directors are sceptical of the boundaries of the new standards while in Portugal they are more positive. The main advantage of the new standards in Portugal, according to the opinion of the respondents, is that the reform makes consolidation of financial statements easier, as with the new standards there will be comparability between financial reporting of local governments and controlled business entities. The Portuguese respondents also value the potential of the new accounting system to increase the quality of financial reporting, transparency, and comparability among entities. However, these are not important benefits for Spanish professionals.

The main challenges and difficulties for implementing IPSAS are similar for both countries, highlighting for example the lack of training in the area and technical support, as well as the lack of adequate information systems. This confirms what previous literature has pointed out concerning the IPSAS implementation (Jorge et al., 2019; Manes Rossi et al., 2016) and should be considered by the European Commission if EPSAS project is finally developed and must be implemented by countries.

The modernization of governmental accounting has led to accrual accounting implementation in most countries, and only a few have maintained the cash accounting system. IPSAS are a clear reference for countries that want to move to accrual accounting, as is the case in Latin-American countries. Furthermore, many countries have adapted their national standards to IPSAS, considering that they are a set of legitimated international standards and that in this case it is easier for accounting standards and also for governments. This is also the case in the European Union, which at the moment considers that IPSAS can be a useful reference to develop EPSAS.

In summary, this chapter shows that modeling national standards after IPSAS does not solve per se the problems of accrual accounting in countries with a legal tradition focusing on the use of cash budgets. The context and institutional elements can also be influencing factors. In fact, this chapter shows differences between Spain and Portugal although there are similarities in the political-administrative system.

This chapter also has limitations, such as different levels of implementation in both countries; in Portugal, most governments are given the first steps in applying the new accounting system because it was foreseen in their application since 2018 for central government and since 2020 for local government. The use of the survey method also has some limitations that should be considered in the analysis. It would be recommendable to repeat the survey after the system has been in effect for two years. Another limitation is that most of the respondents in Spain are from small entities, so the results can have some bias; thus, it is necessary to know the opinion of professionals of bigger entities. Further research should develop a regression model to test the influence of some variables in IPSAS implementation, such as size, cultural aspects and respondents' features, among others.

References

Adhikari, P., & Mellemvik, F. (2010). The adoption of IPSASs in South Asia: A comparative study of seven countries. In M. Tsamenyi & S. Uddin (Eds.), *Research in accounting in emerging economies, 10* (pp. 169–199). Bingley, UK: Emerald Group Publishing Limited.

Argento, D., Peda, P., & Grossi, G. (2018). The enabling role of institutional entrepreneurs in the adoption of IPSAS within a transitional economy: The case of Estonia. *Public Administration and Development, 38*(1), 39–49.

Brusca, I., Caperchione, E., Cohen, S. C., & Manes-Rossi, F. (2015). *Public sector accounting and auditing in Europe: The challenge of harmonization*. London: Palgrave Macmillan.

Brusca, I., & Martínez, J. C. (2016). Adopting international public sector accounting standards: A challenge for modernizing and harmonizing public sector accounting. *International Review of Administrative Sciences, 82*(4), 724–744.

Brusca, I., Montesinos, V., & Chow, D. S. (2013). Legitimating international public sector accounting standards (IPSAS): The case of Spain. *Public Money & Management, 33*(6), 437–444.

Christiaens, J., Vanhee, C., Manes-Rossi, F., Aversano, N., & Van Cauwenberge, P. (2015). The effects of IPSAS on reforming governmental financial reporting: An international comparison. *International Review of Administrative Sciences, 81*(1), 158–177.

Ellwood, S., & Newberry, S. (2007). Public sector accrual accounting: Institutionalising neo-liberal principles? *Accounting, Auditing & Accountability Journal, 20*(4), 549–573.

European Commission. (2013). *Report from the Commission to the Council and the European Parliament. Towards implementing harmonised public sector accounting standards in member states: The suitability of IPSAS for the member states*. Brussels, Belgium: European Commission.

EUROSTAT. (2012). *Overview and comparison of public accounting and auditing practices in the 27 EU Member States*. Retrieved January 2015, from European Commission website: http://ec.europa.eu/eurostat/documents/1015035/4261806/study-on-public-accounting-andauditing-2012.pdf/5ad43e2b-2ba7-4b05-afab-d690fc2ad9dd

Gomes, P., Brusca, I., & Fernandes, M. J. (2019). Implementing the International Public Sector Accounting Standards for consolidated financial statements: Facilitators, benefits and challenges. *Public Money & Management, 39*(8), 544–552.

Gomes, P., Fernandes, M. J., & Carvalho, J. (2015). The international harmonization process of public sector accounting in Portugal: The perspective of different stakeholders. *International Journal of Public Administration, 38*(4), 268–281.

Hood, C. (1995). The "New Public Management" in the 1980s: Variations on a theme. *Accounting, Organizations and Society, 20*(2–3), 93–109.

Hopper, T., Lassoud, P., & Soobaroyen, T. (2017). Globalisation, accounting and developing countries. *Critical Perspectives on Accounting, 43*, 125–148.

Hyndman, N., & Connolly, C. (2011). Accruals accounting in the public sector: A road not always taken. *Management Accounting Research, 22*(1), 36–45.

IMF. (2012). *Fiscal transparency, accountability and Risk*. International Monetary Fund, Fiscal Affairs and Statistics Departments.

Jorge, S., Brusca, I., & Nogueira, S. P. (2019). Translating IPSAS into National Standards: An illustrative comparison between Spain and Portugal. *Journal of Comparative Policy Analysis: Research and Practice, 21*(5), 445–462.

Lapsley, I., Mussari, R., & Paulsson, G. (2009). On the adoption of accrual accounting in the public sector: A self-evident and problematic reform. *European Accounting Review, 18*(4), 719–723.

Manes Rossi, F., Cohen, S., Caperchione, E., & Brusca, I. (2016). Harmonizing public sector accounting in Europe: Thinking out of the box. *Public Money & Management, 36*(3), 189–196.

Oulasvirta, L. O. (2014). Governmental financial accounting and European harmonisation: Case study of Finland. *Accounting, Economics, and Law: A Convivium, 4*(3), 237–263.

Pina, V., Torres, L., & Yetano, A. (2009). Accrual accounting in EU local governments: One method, several approaches. *European Accounting Review, 18*(4), 765–807.

PwC – PricewaterhouseCoopers. (2014, August 1). *Collection of information related to the potential impact, including costs, of implementing accrual accounting in the public sector and technical analysis of the suitability of individual IPSAS standards (2013/S 107-182395)*. Retrieved September 2016, from http://www.pwc.be/en/publications/2014/epsas_oct_2014.pdf

CHAPTER 6

General Conclusions

Patrícia Gomes, Isabel Brusca, Maria José Fernandes, and Vicente Montesinos

Abstract This chapter summarizes the main conclusions obtained in the comparative analysis between Portugal and Spain in relation to the implementation of the IPSAS-based accounting system. The two countries needed important efforts for adapting national standards to IPSAS, which required human and technological resources. The main advantage has been the homogenization between business and governmental accounting

P. Gomes • M. J. Fernandes
Department of Accounting and Taxation, Polytechnic Institute of Cávado and Ave, Barcelos, Portugal
e-mail: pgomes@ipca.pt; mjfernandes@ipca.pt

I. Brusca (✉)
Department of Accounting and Finance, University of Zaragoza, Zaragoza, Spain
e-mail: ibrusca@unizar.es

V. Montesinos
Department of Accounting, University of Valencia, Valencia, Spain
e-mail: Vicente.Montesinos@uv.es

I. Brusca et al. (eds.), *Challenges in the Adoption of International Public Sector Accounting Standards*, Public Sector Financial Management, https://doi.org/10.1007/978-3-030-63125-3_6

standards, making easier the consolidation of financial statements for the public sector. Nevertheless, budgetary reporting is still prepared with the modified cash basis and considered the most useful tool for decision making.

Keywords IPSAS • Portugal • Spain • Comparative analysis

Most countries have carried out important reforms of their public sector accounting systems during recent years, introducing accrual accounting principles and business rationalities. Even though the harmonization of public sector accounting was not considered a main aim until recently, the development of a set of international standards issued by the IPSASB has favoured the process. The fact is that IPSAS have played an important role in the reform processes of governmental accounting in several countries (Brusca & Martínez, 2016; Christiaens, Vanhee, Manes Rossi, Aversano, & Van Cauwenberge, 2015; Gómez & Montesinos, 2012; Manes Rossi, Cohen, Caperchione, & Brusca, 2016), emerging a trend towards the international harmonization of public sector accounting, although in practice there are still several differences between countries (Brusca, Caperchione, Cohen, & Manes-Rossi, 2015).

The literature refers to the potential benefits of IPSAS adoption, such as increasing accountability and transparency, comparability among governments or the legitimacy of the standards and therefore of the governments that implement them. There are however some critics of the IPSAS, arguing for example that the spirit and financial logic of IFRS prevails in IPSAS, incorporating short-term logic and financial performance (Ellwood and Newberry, 2007; Hopper, Lassoud, & Soobaroyen, 2017; Oulasvirta, 2014).

The first chapter of this book summarizes the IPSASB organization and refers to the conceptual framework issued by it. This framework aims to assist the standard setter to develop consistent and relevant standards and, although one of the objectives was to consider the specific features of public sector entities, several critics have emerged because it follows the IASB approach. In fact, some of the IPSAS were developed earlier than the conceptual framework (Christiaens & Neyt, 2015). This has been one of the reasons behind the debate about the convenience of its application.

There are however many arguments in favour of the IPSAS, which are considered an international and widely accepted set of accounting standards. Proponents point out that it is an appropriate mixture of private and public sector principles: while the IPSAS are based as much as possible on well-acknowledged private sector standards, they also reflect necessary public sector particularities. In fact, some scholars (Steccolini, 2019; Van Helden & Reichard, 2016) argue that their structure, completeness and focus on public sector have changed considerably over time. In part due to the influence of some of its members, the IPSASB is now more aware of public sector particularities and issues of "publicness" in comparison with a decade ago. This change is manifested for instance in the fact that the IPSASB has increased the scope of stakeholder consultations.

The second chapter summarizes the position of several countries with respect to the IPSAS, grouping them according to the administrative system. In Anglo-Saxon countries, the homogenization between public and private organizations prevails, and in some cases the IFRS are considered as a reference, so their accounting systems are IPSAS-like. In Napoleonic countries, the situation is more diverse, neither France or Italy have adapted their accounting system to the IPSAS. And the same can be said for Germanic, Nordic and Latin American countries. In each of these groups, there are countries that have been enrolled in the IPSAS network (Jorge, Brusca, & Nogueira, 2019) and others that are more reluctant to adapt to the IPSAS or that have not started a process of reform of governmental accounting. To sum up, the chapter takes stock of the large variations that can be seen in the current state of IPSAS implementation across the globe.

Nevertheless, the literature has shown that accounting harmonization would be desirable, given the need to achieve the comparability of financial reporting among countries, especially in the European Union framework. This need led the European Union to develop a strategy for the harmonization of public sector accounting and the development of a set of European Public Sector Accounting Standards is one of the objectives of the European Commission. IPSAS will be a reference for the European standards but some questions remain, such as to what extent accountants in all of the various public sector organizations across Europe will be able and willing to apply these standards in practice.

As Jorge et al. (2019) point out, a network around the IPSAS has been created and the IPSASB has been the main actor in this process, trying to develop standards that can be applied worldwide. Portugal and Spain are two examples of countries that have joined the network, although with some differences in the process.

Chapters 3 and 4 present the normative process and take stock of the experiences of Spain and Portugal in the adoption of the IPSAS, showing the opinion of practitioners about the appropriateness of the new system for management and accountability purposes, the usefulness and the use of the information produced, as well as the advantages, disadvantages and main challenges for its implementation. Studying the process of public sector accounting change in the context of the Iberian Peninsula provides insights into the reforms carried out in two countries that have undergone significant processes of political, institutional and administrative change over the last three decades (Ongaro, 2008) and that operate in different environments characterized by their legal, political, economic, social and taxation systems. Along with the Napoleonic influence on the political-administrative system of both countries (Ongaro, 2008), there are particular features that condition the relationships between the major actors (agents of change) and their quests for legitimacy (Albu, Albu, & Alexander, 2014). As a consequence, different institutional characteristics led to the decision to introduce IPSAS in these contexts (Brusca, Montesinos, & Chow, 2013; Gomes, Fernandes, & Carvalho, 2015).

Chapter 3 describes the normative process of IPSAS adoption in the Portuguese context as well as the evidence concerning the recent implementation of the new IPSAS-based accounting system. The perspective of different actors involved in the reform, namely pilot entities, standard setters, professionals and Court of Auditors, is also presented.

Being a European continental country, the process of public sector accounting reform in Portugal is embedded in excessive bureaucratic issues and needs to be approved by law, with a weak influence of professionals. Although Portugal has been called a "latecomer" to NPM initiatives, it has more than 20 years of experience using accrual accounting.

The approval of the POCP in 1997 was an important starting point of public sector accounting reform in Portugal. In spite of the limitations identified by entities of central government (Eurostat, 2012), the standard setters and professionals recognize that an important step has been taken. After the adoption of IFRS into the business accounting system in 2010 and the general application of IPSAS worldwide, the Portuguese government felt pressured to implement a new public accounting system. The change to the SNC-AP started in 2011, during the period of economic and financial international crisis under the influence of the Troika, in

2011, which pushed for improvements in accountability in public sector financial management and accounts, including the reformation of the existent public sector accounting system towards the adoption of IPSAS.

Taking into consideration how little time has passed since the approval of SNC-AP, this chapter describes and presents the experience of Portuguese (central and local) entities working with the IPSAS-based accounting system from the perspective of different actors. Pilot entities highlight that the complexity of the new standards requires more support from external supervisors and supporting bodies (like OCC, CNCP, DGO) to help them deal with the main difficulties encountered in the SNC-AP implementation. The lack of human resources with appropriate qualifications with respect to the new public sector accounting standards and the unsuitable software used are also emphasized as important difficulties. The scarce involvement of supporting bodies and the complexity of the system are the most important elements that can explain the relatively low level of the SNC-AP implementation.

From the perspective of other actors, such as auditors, standard setters and preparers/professionals, several advantages and disadvantages of the SNC-AP can be identified. The main advantages include the improvement of accountability, the transparency of public accounts, as well as of the quality of financial reporting, including the elaboration of consolidated statements. The use of the information for accountability purposes and for decision making is also highlighted by them as important advantage of the new accounting and reporting system.

With respect to the difficulties in the SNC-AP implementation we find a high level of coherence in their opinion. The excessive bureaucracy in public administrations, the lack of human resources with expertise in this field and the lack of political involvement and technical support (mainly information systems) have been considered important obstacles for adopting the new IPSAS-based accounting systems. These findings essentially agree with the pilot entities' feedback. In relation to the measures that can be implemented to assure the success of the reform, the professionals highlighted the need to invest in adequate training and human resources, to equip entities with appropriate information systems and to increase the engagement of managers and politicians. These results are very similar to those obtained in the Spanish context.

In Spain, traditionally accounting standards for the public sector have followed the business sector standards. Therefore, the main driver for introducing an accounting system adapted to the IPSAS was the reform of business accounting standards carried out in 2007 through the European Union strategy to apply the IAS and IFRS. In 2010, a new General Governmental Accounting Plan was approved, considering two references: accounting standards for the business sector (based on IFRS) and the International Standards of the IPSASB. Consequently, the Accounting Plan passed in 2010 incorporates most of the accounting principles contained in the IPSAS at that moment, recognizing that the standards have gained legitimacy at international level. The General Government Accounting Plan is an umbrella for all the public sector, but each level of government has an adaptation. Another characteristic of all the levels of governments is that along with the financial accounting system that is adapted to the IPSAS, there is a budgetary accounting system in which the modified cash criteria is maintained.

For the central government the adaptation was approved and applied in 2011 and in 2013 a standard for the elaboration of consolidated statements, compulsory for central government since 2014, was approved. Consolidated statements have been an important challenge derived from the application of the IPSAS.

Regional governments have autonomy to develop their own accounting system and, as a consequence, the adaptation schedules are very diverse. Some regional governments have adapted their standards to the 2010 General Government Accounting Plan and others continue with the old system. This is an example of the heterogeneity of accounting standards between entities even in the same country.

For local governments, the new accounting standards, adapted to IPSAS, were approved in 2013 and have been applied since 2015. As a consequence, the accounting system and the preparation of financial statements are adapted to international standards and their recognition and measurement principles resemble those of the international standards. However, the accounting plan does not include consolidated accounts standards because they are not compulsory for local government. However, consolidated budgets are prepared.

Chapter 4 shows the opinion of preparers of the information about the convenience of the new system and the usefulness of the information prepared for the three levels of government, evidencing some differences between them that can be due to the differences in the context of each level. In central government, the preparers consider that the application of the new system is adequate and fits well into the Spanish context. One of the main advantages of the new system has been the homogenization of criteria for different entities within the central government (administrative organisms, business and non-profit entities, such as foundations), improving the quality of financial reporting and making it easier to elaborate consolidated statements. Both preparers and auditors consider that the new system has improved the quality of financial reporting and that the main use of the information is for accountability purposes. The preparers still value budgetary reporting more than accrual financial reporting.

In regional governments, accounting managers also appreciate the improvement in the quality of the information for accountability purposes. An important advantage, in their opinion, is the homogenization between entities, which makes the consolidation of the financial statements easier. Among the difficulties of the new model the accounting managers highlight the lack of means and technical support, as well as the lack of political participation and interest, and the excessive bureaucracy in the public administration. The respondents from regional governments also rate budgetary reporting more highly.

In the local governments, the accountants and financial managers appreciate more budgetary reporting than accrual financial statements. One of the main reasons is that the laws require the use of budgetary information for different purposes, such as the control of budgetary stability, while the use of accrual reporting is not required for management or decision-making purposes. In this framework, the financial directors consider that the information is mainly used for accountability purposes and the audit institutions (central and regional) are considered the main user of the information. The consolidation of financial statements is voluntary for accrual accounting and a high percentage of respondents consider consolidated reporting useful, but there are still many financial directors that do not consider it important in the local government context.

Chapter 5 compares the situation in both countries, analysing differences in the normative process. The comparative analysis of the opinion of practitioners is focused on local government. Spain began adapting governmental accounting to the IPSAS in 2010 and the application in local government took place in 2015, while in Portugal the process started in 2015 and some preparatory work was done before its application. For example, some pilot entities were used to check the system and to legitimize it. This may be one of the main reasons for the differences in the opinion of accounting managers in the two countries.

The analysis carried out for Portugal and Spain shows that there are differences in the opinion of the professionals of local governments in the two countries about the appropriateness of the reform. In Spain, financial directors are sceptical with the boundaries of the new standards, while in Portugal they are more positive. The main benefit of the new standards in Portugal, according to the respondents, is that the reform makes the consolidation of financial statements easier, because with the new standards, there will be comparability between the financial reporting of the local governments and their controlled business entities. However, these are not important benefits in the opinion of Spanish professionals. Local governments do not prepare consolidated reporting and because of this, this advantage is not relevant. The Portuguese respondents also value the potential of the new system to increase the quality of financial reporting, its transparency and the comparability among entities.

The main challenges to and difficulties for implementing the IPSAS are similar in both countries, the preparers highlighted for example the lack of human resources training, of technical support and of adequate information systems. This confirms previous literature (Manes Rossi et al., 2016) and should be taken into account by the European Commission when developing the EPSAS and a strategy to implement them.

To sum up, the IPSAS have been adopted by many countries worldwide and the mimetic effect has had an important effect in European continental countries like Portugal and Spain. Their adoption would lead to the comparability of financial reporting in the international field. In the case of Spain and Portugal, the reform of business accounting system based on IFRS and the institutional context (especially in the Portuguese case due to the external pressures of the International Monetary Fund) played an important role in the public sector accounting changes (Gomes et al., 2015; Gomes, Brusca, & Fernandes, 2019).

References

Albu, C. N., Albu, N., & Alexander, D. (2014). When global accounting standards meet the local context—Insights from an emerging economy. *Critical Perspectives on Accounting, 25*(6), 489–510.

Brusca, I., Caperchione, E., Cohen, S. C., & Manes-Rossi, F. (2015). *Public sector accounting and auditing in Europe: The challenge of harmonization*. London: Palgrave Macmillan.

Brusca, I., & Martínez, J. C. (2016). Adopting international public sector accounting standards: A challenge for modernizing and harmonizing public sector accounting. *International Review of Administrative Sciences, 82*(4), 724–744.

Brusca, I., Montesinos, V., & Chow, D. S. (2013). Legitimating international public sector accounting standards (IPSAS): the case of Spain. *Public Money & Management, 33*(6), 437–444.

Christiaens, J., & Neyt, S. (2015). International public sector accounting standards. In T. Budding, G. Grossi, & T. Tagesson (Eds.), *Public sector accounting* (pp. 23–62). London: Routledge.

Christiaens, J., Vanhee, C., Manes Rossi, F., Aversano, N., & Van Cauwenberge, P. (2015). The effect of IPSAS on reforming governmental financial reporting: An international comparison. *International Review of Administrative Sciences, 81*(1), 158–177.

Ellwood, S., & Newberry, S. (2007). Public sector accrual accounting: Institutionalising neo-liberal principles? *Accounting, Auditing & Accountability Journal, 20*(4), 549–573.

EUROSTAT, (2012). *Overview and comparison of public accounting and auditing practices in the 27 EU Member States.* Available in: https://ec.europa.eu/eurostat/documents/1015035/4261806/study-on-public-accounting-and-auditing-2012.pdf/5ad43e2b-2ba7-4b05-afab-d690fc2ad9dd

Gomes, P., Brusca, I., & Fernandes, M. J. (2019). Implementing the International Public Sector Accounting Standards for consolidated financial statements: Facilitators, benefits and challenges. *Public Money & Management, 39*(8), 544–552.

Gomes, P., Fernandes, M. J., & Carvalho, J. (2015). The international harmonization process of public sector accounting in Portugal: The perspective of different stakeholders. *International Journal of Public Administration, 38*(4), 268–281.

Gómez, M. G., & Montesinos, V. (2012). Las innovaciones en contabilidad gubernamental en Latinoamérica: el caso de Colombia. *INNOVAR. Revista de Ciencias Administrativas y Sociales, 22*(45), 17–35.

Hopper, T., Lassoud, P., & Soobaroyen, T. (2017). Globalisation, accounting and developing countries. *Critical Perspectives on Accounting, 43*, 125–148.

Jorge, S., Brusca, I., & Nogueira, S. P. (2019). Translating IPSAS into National Standards: An illustrative comparison between Spain and Portugal. *Journal of Comparative Policy Analysis: Research and Practice.* https://doi.org/10.1080/13876988.2019.157997.

Manes Rossi, F., Cohen, S., Caperchione, E., & Brusca, I. (2016). Harmonizing public sector accounting in Europe: Thinking out of the box. *Public Money & Management, 36*(3), 189–196.

Ongaro, E. (2008). Introduction: The reform of public management in France, Greece, Italy, Portugal and Spain. *International Journal of Public Sector Management, 21*(2), 101–117.

Oulasvirta, L. (2014). The reluctance of a developed country to choose International Public Sector Accounting Standards of the IFAC. A critical case study. *Critical Perspectives on Accounting, 25*(3), 272–285.

Steccolini, I. (2019). Accounting and the post-new public management: Re-considering publicness in accounting research. *Accounting, Auditing & Accountability Journal, 32*(1), 255–279.

Van Helden, J., & Reichard, C. (2016). Commonalities and differences in public and private sector performance management practices: A literature review. In M. J. Epstein, F. Verbeeten, & S. K. Widener (Eds.), *Performance measurement and management control: Contemporary issues* (pp. 309–351). Bingley, UK: Emerald.

Index

I. Brusca et al. (eds.), *Challenges in the Adoption of International Public Sector Accounting Standards*, Public Sector Financial Management, https://doi.org/10.1007/978-3-030-63125-3

The manufacturer's authorised representative in the EU is Springer Nature Customer Service Centre GmbH, Europaplatz 3, 69115 Heidelberg, Germany. If you have any concerns regarding our products, please contact ProductSafety@springernature.com

Printed and bound by CPI Group (UK) Ltd, Croydon, CR0 4YY
25/09/2026
02223153-0003